Have You Heard...?

Listening Comprehension

Mary Underwood

Oxford University Press

Oxford University Press, Walton Street, Oxford OX2 6DP

LONDON GLASGOW NEW YORK TORONTO
DELHI BOMBAY CALCUTTA MADRAS KARACHI
KUALA LUMPUR SINGAPORE HONG KONG TOKYO
NAIROBI DAR ES SALAAM CAPE TOWN SALISBURY
MELBOURNE AUCKLAND

and associates in
BEIRUT BERLIN IBADAN MEXICO CITY NICOSIA

ISBN 0 19 457030 4 Classroom Edition
ISBN 0 19 457031 2 Intensive Study Edition

ⒸOxford University Press 1979

First published 1979
Third impression 1982

Set in Monophoto Plantin and Univers
by Filmtype Services Limited, Scarborough.
Printed in Hong Kong by Hing Yip Printing Co.

Contents

Introduction

Have You Heard . . .? is a set of twenty units of aural
comprehension practice. Each unit consists of three short
listening passages with additional material and exercises based
on each one. The units are intended for lower level students,
who may have studied English in their own country for two or
three years or spent a short time studying in England. They
are particularly useful to the student who has little
opportunity to hear English speakers, and are designed to
prepare students to go on to the intermediate level aural
comprehension books, *Listen to This!* and *What a Story!* (by
the same author and published by Oxford University Press).

The Aim
The *aim* of these units is to teach students to listen effectively
and to enable them to select the information they require from
what they hear. The emphasis is on the student's role as
'listener'. The use of real (unscripted) speech gives students
the opportunity to experience the ordinary, everyday language
of the native speaker, which they are unlikely to find in the
usual class situation, where they probably meet a more
deliberately patterned type of language.

The Material
There are two tapes containing, in all, sixty extracts from
recorded conversations (three per unit). Each extract is
between one and two minutes in length.

The number of speakers in each extract varies, but the same
speakers recur frequently through the recordings so that the
problems of listening are reduced as the student becomes
familiar with some of the voices.

The speakers come from various parts of the British Isles so
the student has the opportunity to hear a selection of voices
and accents; see *The people you hear* on pages 6–7, where
regional accents are noted. However, none of the accents is
very marked, and students at this level should not experience
particular difficulty.

1

The order of the units has been determined by the degree of difficulty the student is likely to experience in listening to them, from the point of view of content, vocabulary, accent, speed and so on. The Contents List indicates not only the title of each unit (which is most helpful to those using the book in conjunction with other functional material) but also the title of each extract (which is more indicative of the topic and helps the teacher doing topic-based work).

The exercises are designed to train the student to listen 'extensively', in order to grasp the main information content of the conversations, and sometimes 'intensively', looking for the detailed meaning of an utterance. Through listening and doing the exercises, students will become sensitive to the way in which speakers use language for various purposes and at the end of each unit they are invited, in the '*Can you say . . .?*' section, to try to use some of the language they have heard for a similar purpose.

The *Classroom Edition* of *Have You Heard . . .?* contains all the work material for each of the units: the list of relevant words and phrases from the tapes, the introductory paragraph, the 'Points of Detail', and the exercises. It does *not* contain the answers or the tapescript.

The *Intensive Study Edition* contains *all* the material of the *Classroom Edition* as well as the answers and the tapescript.

Using the Tapes and the Book

1   The *words and phrases* used to express the particular function in the conversations are listed in the '*They say . . .*' section which is placed at the beginning of each unit for easy reference. It includes the utterances which speakers in the three recorded extracts have used to do whatever is indicated in the unit title (e.g. agreeing and disagreeing) and which may be used or adapted by the students when they try to carry out a similar activity. Teachers may wish to discuss these words and phrases with their students before listening to the conversations, but they may find it more valuable to discuss them after working through the recordings when the context of each one will have become apparent. The words and phrases are listed in the order in which they will be heard, so that a teacher who only wants to use one of the three recordings can easily identify the relevant phrases.

2

2   Each section of each unit can be used independently. Each is devised according to the same pattern (although the type of exercise varies). The teacher can, therefore, expect to spend a similar length of time on any section, and, if time is limited, can work on each section on a different occasion. Having completed the three sections of a unit, the learner will then be ready to tackle the 'Can you say . . .?' exercise at the end of the unit.

Working through a Section

3   The *brief introductory paragraph* at the beginning of the section should be read before the tape is listened to, as it will give the listener some guidance on what to expect on the tape.

4   The *Points of Detail* should be checked through carefully before listening to the tape. These fairly extensive notes are designed to prepare students for the listening activity by familiarizing them with some of the words and expressions which they will hear on the tape and which may cause them difficulty. (Words which have a straightforward dictionary definition are not included, and can be found by referring to a good monolingual dictionary such as A. S. Hornby's *Oxford Advanced Learners Dictionary of Current English* or the same author's *Oxford Student's Dictionary of Current English*.)

5   The *tape* should then be listened to carefully, preferably without stopping. This gives students the opportunity to accustom themselves to the voices and to get some idea of the content of the conversation. As the extracts are quite short, some students may wish to repeat this first run-through. It is important for students to try to follow the overall gist of what they hear at this stage and to become accustomed to being unperturbed if they fail to understand some parts.

6   At this stage, some teachers may wish to discuss the content of what has just been listened to with the students, to check that they have understood the main points.

7   The *exercises* form the next part of each section. The 'true/false' and *multiple-choice* type exercises will necessitate returning to the tape to find the answers, as will a number of the other exercises. The exercises marked with outline headphones (⌾) are those which cannot be completed without close reference to the recorded extracts. Those marked with

solid headphones (🎧) are exercises which are recorded on the tape straight after the extract to which they refer. In some situations, it might be easier to do the latter type of exercise first (while still in the language laboratory, for example) and leave the former until later.

8   How 'complete' the students' answers will be will depend on a number of factors: (a) their ability to find the answers; (b) what the teacher demands of them, bearing in mind that the aim of many of the exercises is to develop the skill of understanding, not the skill of composing written answers; and (c) whether they are able to control the tape independently of other students (i.e. whether they are alone in a language laboratory or at home, or whether they are members of a class or group with a single tape-recorder).

9   The exercises are designed for individual use, but they can be used in groups or with partners to provide more oral practice.

10 It is important that the exercises should *not* be treated as *test items*. They are designed as aids to aural comprehension practice, directing the students' attention to 'focal points' on the tape so that they will learn to listen more effectively.

11 The student should ideally be able to seek *advice and guidance* from their teacher at any time while they are carrying out the exercises.

12 To bridge the gap between the three sections of a unit and the *'Can you say . . .?'* exercise at the end of each unit, students may find it helpful to re-enact the conversation they have just heard, endeavouring to include some of the phrases used by the speakers. At a more elementary level, straightforward repetition of a few utterances selected by the teacher may be more appropriate.

Using the 'Can you say . . .?' Exercise

13 Having completed the three sections of a unit, students are now ready to try the *'Can you say . . .?'* exercise. For this activity, they will need to belong to a group or, at least, to have a partner to work with.
This section is designed to give learners an *immediate opportunity* to practise using and responding to the kind of language they have just heard in the recorded conversations.

The extent to which this exercise is exploited will depend on the ability of the students and the wishes of the teacher and students. It need not be developed in too much detail, but should be used to give students confidence in handling the language they have been listening to on the tape.

Acknowledgements

Photographs by

Michael Copsey, Units 13, 14; Julian Essam, 6, 18, 19; Stuart Franklin, 2, 4; Judith Hansell, 12; Tim Hinton, 1, 15, 16, 17; Ray Issler, 5; Geraint Jones, 8; Andy Lane, 3; Chris Nissen, 9; Jacqui Oldfield, 10, 13; Gary Summons, 11; Martin Urmson, 7, 20.

I would like to thank the many people who allowed me to record their conversations. My particular thanks are due to Mrs Joan Ager who gave valuable assistance with the transcription of the taped material, and to my husband and my daughter, Sarah, who spent a great deal of time helping with recording and transcribing the taped material as well as checking the manuscript.

London, September 1978   Mary Underwood

The people you hear

Alec	a librarian
Avril	a sixth-form school-girl, a friend of Sarah and Lucy
Beryl	a lecturer in psychology
Bob	a lecturer in education
Celia	a special projects officer concerned with industrial language training
Chris	a student; from Sheffield
Colin	an artist; Moira's husband; a Scotsman
Doris	a housewife; Laurie's wife; from the border of England and Scotland
Felix	a teacher of physics
Frank	a sociologist; Liz's husband; originally from Durham
Graham	the manager of an electrical wholesale company; Tim O.'s brother; a friend of Nigel; from Southampton
Isabel	a teacher; Ray's wife; a friend and colleague of Julia
Jeremy	a member of the Royal Air Force; a friend of Susan
John	a teacher of physics; Mary's husband
Jonathon	a student of economics
Julia	a teacher; a friend and colleague of Isabel
Laurie	a retired factory worker; Doris's husband
Liz	a librarian; Frank's wife
Lucy	a sixth-form school-girl; a friend of Avril and Sarah
Mary	the author; John's wife
Matthew	a play group leader; Lucy's brother
Maureen	a student of economics; from Bristol
Moira	an artist; Colin's wife; a Scot
Nigel	an articled clerk to a solicitor; a friend of Graham and Tim O.; from Southampton
Ray	a professional cook; Isabel's husband; a native of Ireland
Sarah	a sixth-form school-girl; daughter of John and Mary; Susan's sister; a friend of Avril and Lucy

Scilla	a part-time lecturer in English
Simon	a lecturer in English
Susan	a medical student; daughter of John and Mary; Sarah's sister
Tim C.	a lecturer in Spanish
Tim O.	a storeman in a pipe and fittings company; Graham's brother; a friend of Nigel; from Southampton
Tom J.	the director of a national centre concerned with industrial language training
Tom M.	a retired farmer; Win's husband; living in Devon
Verity	an engineering student; a friend of Susan
Win	a housewife; Tom M.'s wife; living in Devon

1 People talking about the things they like

> **They say . . .**
>
> I enjoy it
> I enjoy the company
>
> I would be happy to spend every future holiday . . .
> Do you like mountains?
> The Pyrenees are great for walking
> I'd be much happier knowing . . .
>
> lovely things
> They love doing . . .
> That's what's so marvellous about . . .
> They want to do it
> They're more fun
> Do you like to . . .?
> I like doing . . .
> I thoroughly enjoy it

1.1 Felix talks about his job as a school-master.

Felix shows his pleasure by mentioning the good things
about his job. He begins by saying that he decided quite
quickly about what he wanted to do as a job.

Points of detail
no great lengthy process — Felix did not take a long time to decide.
staff — here, teachers in the school
a structured system — an organized arrangement
boss — one's superior at work
in the same boat — usually meaning 'having the same difficulties',
    but Felix means simply 'in the same situation'
work-mates — people you work with. Another example is 'class-
    mates' i.e. people in the same class as you.
age-groups — here, boys who work together because they are
    about the same age

🎧 **Exercise 1**

Listen carefully to what Felix says and decide which of the following statements is true and which is false.

1 It took Felix a very long time to choose a job.
2 Felix believes he chose the right job.
3 The system Felix works in is very structured, with each person being someone else's boss.
4 Each group of boys is taught by only one teacher.
5 Felix says his job is like working in an office.
6 Felix would like a different job.
7 Felix has to do the same things every day.
8 Felix teaches boys of different ages.

🎧 **Exercise 2**

Find a word or phrase on the tape which means the same as each of the words or phrases in italics below.

1 *Making up his mind*
2 I've made *an error*
3 *fellow workers*
4 work with *each other*
5 *in contrast to* an office situation
6 in *an annual* situation

🎧 **Exercise 3**

Listen to Exercise 3 on your tape. Write down what Felix says. You will need to stop the tape to give yourself time to write. Don't include the hesitations and little corrections he makes.

🎧 **Exercise 4**

Make a list of all the words Felix uses which refer to people of some sort, e.g. friends. You should find five or six.

1.2 Matthew talks about mountain holidays.

Matthew is sure that he likes the mountains in Wales better than any of the other mountains which Moira and Colin mention to him. This is because he is more interested in walking in the mountains than in ski-ing or climbing.

10

Points of detail

Snowdonia — a mountainous region in North Wales which includes Mount Snowdon (1085 m)

the Alps — the highest mountain range in Europe, running from South Eastern France through Switzerland and Northern Italy to Austria

the Pyrenees — the mountains along the border between France and Spain

great — very good indeed

2,900 feet high — approximately 884 metres

beside the point — here, not important

an Alp — It is not normal to use 'Alp' in the singular, but Matthew uses it to refer to a single mountain in the Alps.

Exercise 1

Having heard the tape, try to answer each of the following questions briefly. You may need to listen again to find the answers.

1 Does Matthew like all mountains?
2 What does he think the Swiss Alps are good for?
3 What, in his view, are the Swiss Alps not good for?
4 Does Matthew think the Pyrenees are good for walking?
5 How long does it take to go up and down a Welsh mountain?
6 What would Matthew find embarrassing?

Exercise 2

Complete the following, having looked at the example.
Example: The Swiss mountains are in Switzerland.

1 The Welsh mountains are in . . . .
2 The . . . . mountains are in Italy.
3 The . . . . mountains are in Japan.
4 The Austrian mountains are in . . . .
5 The . . . . mountains are in Greece.
6 The . . . . mountains are in Canada.
7 The Scottish mountains are in . . . .
8 The . . . . mountains are in Norway.

Exercise 3

Use each of the following words and phrases in italics in a sentence of your own to show that you understand what it means. You will find each one on the tape.

1 *I would be happy to* spend
2 I could live there *for ever*
3 Do you like mountains *generally?*
4 they're *no use for* walking
5 if you start *half-way up*
6 you've *achieved* something
7 climbing an Alp *in a day*
8 I haven't *actually* been
9 *embarrassing*
10 who knows England *better than you do*

1.3 Tom J. talks about entertaining small children.

Tom is the father of two small children. He regrets that he is often too busy to spend time with his family and so when he does have time to spare he enjoys doing absolutely anything with his children. Sarah and Simon are interested in how Tom and his children enjoy themselves together.

Points of detail
as far as I'm concerned — meaning 'in my case', 'for me'
Mind you — a kind of warning remark, to show that what you have just said doesn't always apply, e.g. 'I'll help you today. Mind you, I won't always help you.'
outdoor — things done outside, not in the house
for hours on end — for many hours
all the holidays — here, Tom means all the school holidays.
Cressida — Tom's wife. Cressida is an uncommon name.
over-organize — organize too much. The prefix 'over' can be used with many verbs to have this kind of meaning, e.g. over-eat, over-simplify.

Exercise 1

Answer each of the following questions by choosing the right answer from A B C or D.

1   Tom thinks his holidays are
   A too long   C too busy
   B too frequent   D too infrequent
   for him to have time to entertain his children as much as he
   would like to.

2   Children want to do things with their parents if
   A the parents are marvellous
   B the parents are enthusiastic
   C the things to do are lovely
   D the parents don't want to do them

3   Tom thinks it is
   A necessary   C not necessary
   B supposed to be necessary D not fun
   to do outdoor things with children.

4   Simon thinks children sleep better at night
   A if they're exhausted
   B if they're awake for hours on end
   C if they do important things
   D if they play at bedtime

5   Tom spends
   A all the holidays   C Cressida's holidays
   B part of the holidays   D no holidays
   with his children.

6   Tom plays with his children
   A less than his wife does
   B about as much as his wife does
   C when his wife refuses to play with them
   D more than his wife does

7   Simon believes that children
   A can't amuse themselves
   B need organizing all the time
   C don't need organizing all the time
   D should be organized for a long, long time

8 Tom seems
   A to find children tiring
   B to find holidays tiring
   C to organize his children all the time
   D to like children

Exercise 2

*Find a word or phrase in the discussion for which each of the
following words or phrases in italics is an explanation.*

1 that's what so *delightful* about them
2 if you're *keen*
3 they're more *enjoyable*
4 to *tire* them *out*
5 they won't *stop you sleeping*
6 they do need *clearly* to do something
7 something which *uses up energy*
8 organize children *so much*
9 children can *entertain themselves*
10 amuse themselves very well *for ages*

Exercise 3

*List all the specific activities which Tom says he enjoys doing
with his children. You should find six.*

Exercise 4

*Now list ten other ways in which you would entertain small
children.*

Can you say . . .?

Look back at the list of expressions which the speakers used. Using some of the words and expressions you have heard, talk about the things you like. It is important that, like the speakers on the tape, you choose appropriate words and use the kind of intonation which will help to convey the idea of 'liking' this or that.

You might like to use some of the following topics, but choose your own if you prefer.
What you like:
— about your home
— about being a student
— about a book/film/record
— about your job
— about your friends

2 People asking for and giving information

They say . . .

Is he good?
What's special . . .?
Eduardo has only one style
I live in Teddington
Where do you have . . .?
I go to Simone
When you say . . . you mean . . .?
How much do you pay?

The rooms are so big
Is it well furnished?
There's enough . . .
Do you have . . .?
We don't use it
We have . . .
What do you do . . .?
Bridget's got work to do
Don't you find that . . .?
We play . . .
What television programmes would you watch?
Is there a lot . . .?

What's his job?
He's . . .
That's the name of . . .
What does that involve?
It involves . . .
Does he have . . .?
He's paid . . .
They buy . . .
Do they have to buy . . .?
People are . . .
They haven't got . . .

2.1 Beryl and Tim C. discuss hairdressers.

Mary wants to find a good hairdresser. Beryl and Tim give
her information about the hairdressers they use. Many
hairdressers in England use foreign names – here, Vincenzo
and Eduardo, and Simone.

Points of detail

to a larger extent than — more than
I've come across — I've met by chance
style — here, way of doing hair
puts everyone — here, gives everyone
middle-aged — not young, not old. Probably the usual meaning is
    between 40 and 60 years old, but this varies with who is using
    the phrase!
Teddington — a small town to the south west of London
Ealing — a London suburb
chap — a colloquial word for 'man'
nice and easy — 'nice and' is used in front of an adjective to give
    emphasis to the adjective, e.g. 'nice and warm', 'nice and
    comfortable'.
appeal — ask specially
to drop in — to go in without making an appointment
a meeting — used in the business sense, when a number of people
    meet to discuss particular matters. 'Meeting' is not often used
    when one person has an arrangement to meet another socially;
    this would usually be an 'appointment'.
a shampoo and set — a wash followed by curling, drying and
    arranging
a blow dry — Sometimes, people dry their hair with a hair-dryer
    brushing it into the shape they want at the same time.
two-fifty — two pounds fifty pence
a tip — extra money given directly to the person who offers you a
    service, e.g. in a restaurant, to a taxi-driver, to a porter, but not, in
    Britain, in a cinema

Exercise 1

*Give a brief answer to each of the following questions. You
may need to listen to the tape again.*

1 Why does Beryl like her present hairdresser?
2 Which is the elder of the two hairdressers called Vincenzo
   and Eduardo?
3 Why does Beryl think Eduardo isn't a very good hairdresser?
4 Why does Tim say he's surprised that Beryl has her hair done
   in Teddington?

5 Where is Tim's hairdresser's shop?
6 Does Beryl know Tim's hairdresser?
7 When does Beryl go to Simone to have her hair done?
8 Does Beryl know what Simone's prices are?

🎧 Exercise 2

Find a word or phrase from the tape for which each of the following words or phrases in italics is an explanation.

1 And is he *exceptionally* good?
2 very *rare*
3 young, middle-aged or *elderly*
4 Quite *surprising* you go . . .
5 *From time to time* I go . . .
6 I go to Simone *in a rush*
7 *normally* a very quick blow dry
8 I paid *approximately* two-fifty

Exercise 3

Use each of the phrases in italics in a sentence of your own.

1 *the thing I like about* him is . . .
2 I've *come across*
3 *I used to* go to Vincenzo
4 *whether* you're young, middle-aged *or* old
5 quite *amazing* you go . . .
6 the *chap* opposite College
7 easy just to *drop in*
8 *occasionally* I go to Simone
9 I have a *meeting*
10 *I can't remember what* I pay

🎧 Exercise 4

Listen to Exercise 4 on your tape and fill in the blanks below.

I . . . . go to Vincenzo and Eduardo
and. . . . . Eduardo, the . . . . . . one, has only one
style . . . ., and he puts . . . . . . into that . . . . . .,
. . . . you're . . . ., ... or old.'

2.2 Graham tells Sarah something about his attitude to television.

Graham and Bridget live in a rented flat. They are busy young people and so Graham finds that television is a waste of time. Sarah clearly believes that there are advantages to watching television.

Points of detail

T.V. — a common abbreviation for 'television'

He provides it — 'He', here, refers to the landlord from whom Graham and Bridget rent the flat.

Nigel — a friend of Graham's

blasting — Usually 'blasting' means using explosives (for example, in a coal-mine) but here, Graham means 'making a lot of noise'.

scrounge — to get something for nothing, e.g. 'He's always scrounging meals from us. He really ought to learn to cook for himself.'

Scrabble — a well-known word game

endlessly — without end, so here, for a lot of time

a pack of cards — i.e. a complete set of playing cards

Wow! — an exclamation of surprise

extravagant — using money wastefully. Sarah is being ironic.

thirty-two pence — i.e. the pack cost 32p

go out of our way — make a special effort, e.g. 'I'd help her if she asked me to, but I wouldn't go out of my way to offer help.'

feature films — full-length films

documentaries — films made to give a description of some human or social activity (e.g. the way animals live in the jungle, how medical services are organized)

for her geography — because Bridget is a student of geography

such and such — a particular one which is not named at the time of speaking because it is not important, e.g. 'He kept talking about his holidays. He'd been to such and such a place and seen such and such a castle.'

on the box — a slang expression meaning 'on television'

Exercise 1

Decide whether each of the following statements is true or false, according to the conversation.

1 The landlord provides television.
2 Nigel is the landlord.
3 Graham thinks television is a waste of time.
4 Bridget has nothing to do in the evening.
5 Graham likes reading.
6 Graham and Bridget work together all day.

7 Graham thinks that the cards he bought were expensive.
8 Bridget always does as her lecturers tell her.

Exercise 2

Give a word or phrase opposite in meaning to each of the following words and phrases in italics.

1 The rooms are so *big*.
2 Is it *well furnished*?
3 Nigel's *old* television
4 You're not *interested* in . . .
5 It's much *happier*
6 there's always *somebody*
7 Bridget's got *plenty of* work
8 We can *go out*
9 We *bought* a pack of cards
10 Is there *a lot* . . .?

Exercise 3

Make a list of topics about which a documentary film for television could be made. Try to think of at least ten, and list them in the same way as the examples below.
Examples: 1. about the history of aeroplanes
2. about working in a coal-mine
3. . . . .

Exercise 4

Make eight statements about television with which other people might agree.
Example: 1. It's a waste of time.
2. . . . .

2.3 Matthew's sister, Lucy, explains Matthew's job.

Matthew has an unusual job. He works in a playground for children and, in addition to supervising the children, he must find new activities for them. Sarah and Avril ask Lucy a lot of questions because they can't imagine how Matthew spends his time.

Points of detail

officially — Matthew works for the local council and is employed 'officially', i.e. by the local authority, as an Assistant Play Leader.

theatre work-shops — organizing activities related to drama — acting, painting scenery, writing plays, etc.

adventure playgrounds — special areas reserved for children in which various exciting activities are available

sponsored — i.e. supported financially, paid for

Hammersmith Council — the local government (consisting of elected members) in the West London area called Hammersmith

longer term – over a longer period, e.g. 'I'm going to work for the next six weeks, but I have no plans for the longer term.'

by the week — each week

fill out forms — write down the information asked for. Lucy uses 'fill out' which is rather American; most English people say 'fill in a form'.

paid back — i.e. repaid, given money to replace the money they have spent

have an eye for — be a good judge of

railway sleepers — the large pieces of wood used to hold the rails of a railway line

picking things up — here, getting things for nothing or at very little cost

firms — companies, businesses

truck — lorry

leap in it — more usually 'get in it' or even 'jump in it'

telegraph poles — the long pieces of wood (poles) which are used to hold up the telephone wires

play-ey structures — 'Structures' here means pieces of apparatus, things for the children to climb on/in/through, etc. Sarah invents the adjective 'play-ey' to mean 'suitable for play'.

cat-walks — high narrow places where children would have to balance carefully, like a cat on a narrow wall

tyres — the rubber covering of car or lorry wheels

an age limit — a minimum or a maximum age

discipline — keeping order, making people do as he wants them to

six foot three — i.e. six foot three inches tall (approximately two metres)

Exercise 1

Answer each of the following questions. You will find the information you need for the answers on the tape.

1 Who is responsible for financing playgrounds?
2 How often is Matthew paid?
3 Name three things which Matthew might pick up for use in his playground.

4   Are people generous about giving things to the playground?
5   How often can Matthew and his colleagues use the council lorry?
6   What do the play leaders do with the things they pick up?
7   What does Sarah suggest they might do with tyres?
8   Is there an age limit for the children who go to the playground?
9   How old is Matthew?
10 Lucy suggests that Matthew doesn't have any discipline problems at the playground. Why not?

Exercise 2

Find a word or phrase from the conversation for which each of the following words or phrases in italics is an explanation.

1   the *entire* thing
2   a weekly *amount* of money
3   *I understand*
4   they have to *complete* forms
5   they get *repaid* by the Council
6   that *kind* of thing
7   Wood, *etcetera*
8   Do they get *a lot* for nothing?
9   *cut* them up
10 *a large quantity* of tyres

Exercise 3

Listen to Exercise 3 on your tape and write down exactly what Lucy says. You will need to stop your tape to give yourself time to write.

Exercise 4

Make a list of six things that you might 'pick up' and use as part of an adventure playground. Then write a sentence like those in the examples below, saying what to make with each thing you pick up.
Examples: *Wood* is good for making boxes.
            Branches are useful for making places to hide.

Can you say . . .?

Now try to ask for and give information yourself. You will need someone to work with. Use some of the expressions from the list at the beginning of this Unit. Try to give factual information, although it is not always easy to separate facts from opinions. Here are some topics you might like to use:
— somebody's job
— the weather
— a new invention
— everyday habits
— information in a guide book/an advertisement

3 People telling stories

They say . . .

It was . . .
I had one appointment
These appointments were . . .
I got on the Underground
We stopped
We were there . . .
The English didn't . . .
I didn't give up my seat

He said to me that he came . . .
He felt so ill . . .
When I came home . . .
I said, 'You can't go to work . . .'
He went . . .
I said, 'What are you going to do . . .?'

We were sitting . . .
Then we had a breakfast of . . .
The wind dropped

3.1 Tom J. tells the story of how he was delayed on the Underground.

Tom had obviously planned his day very carefully because he had a lot of things to do. Unfortunately, his plans were ruined by a delay on the Underground. He tells his story in such a way that Sarah and Simon can imagine how unpleasant it must have been.

Points of detail
Underground — The underground railway system in London is
    called the Underground or, more colloquially, the Tube.
appointment — arrangement to meet somebody
Pathway — the language centre where Tom works
I reckoned — I believed, I thought

timed it — arranged his time-table for the day
Hounslow West — a station on the Underground to the west of London
Green Park — an underground station in central London
Hyde Park Corner — another central London Underground station near Green Park
50 yards — a little less than 50 metres
tantalizingly — irritatingly
reacted — showed their feelings
give up my seat — offer my seat to somebody else

Exercise 1

Answer each of the following questions by listening carefully to the story. Use a complete sentence for each answer.

1 How many appointments did Tom have in town?
2 At what time did Tom intend to leave central London?
3 How did Tom plan to travel from Hounslow West station to Pathway?
4 Where did he get on the Underground to start his journey to Pathway?
5 Did the train stop before or after Hyde Park station?
6 Tom wasn't sure why the train had stopped. What does he say might have been the reason?
7 For about how long was the train delayed?
8 What did the foreign passengers do when the train was delayed?
9 Why didn't the English passengers say anything?
10 Were all the passengers sitting down?

Exercise 2

Write Tom's diary of plans for the day, beginning:

9.00 a.m. Mr Jones (Insurance) at Central London office.

You will have to invent names and places for all Tom's appointments.

Exercise 3

Use each of the words or phrases in italics in a sentence of your own to show that you know what they mean. They are all taken from the conversation.

1 it was a *very busy* day

26

2 I *reckoned*
3 These appointments were *in town*.
4 I *timed* it . . .
5 I *got on* the Underground
6 We *moved along* to Hyde Park Corner
7 a train stopped *in front of* us
8 *tantalizingly*
9 *typically* English
10 I didn't *give up* my seat

 Exercise 4

Listen carefully to Exercise 4 on your tape and write down exactly what Tom says.

3.2 Doris talks about the time when her son became very ill.

Edward, called Ed by his family, was a young working man when he suddenly became seriously ill. His mother remembers the day when it all started and tells her friends about the difficulty she had in persuading Ed to go to the doctor. Luckily, her son-in-law, Len, was at the house and helped her to get Ed to the hospital.

Points of detail
at Carol's — Doris was visiting her daughter, Carol.
shivering — shaking, usually from cold or from having a fever
ages — a very long time
dreadful — here, very ill indeed
I shall bring the doctor — Doris comes from the North of England, near the border with Scotland, where some people use the verb 'bring' to mean 'fetch'.
wouldn't have made it — To 'make it' is a colloquial way of saying 'manage to do it'.
that was it — that was the end of the matter
anaemia, anaemic — lack of red cells in the blood, causing the person to become weak
I fancy — here, I suppose, I think
Kingston — a town on the Thames to the south west of London
keep you in — here, keep you at the hospital
was sitting — meaning 'was sitting down in the house'
have a word with — speak to
got stuck — here, was kept

Exercise 1

Answer each of the following questions by choosing the right answer from A B C or D.

1   Ed left work and went
   A to Carol's   C to his home
   B to the local garage   D to someone else's house

2   When his mother came home, he said to her
   A 'I'm all right now'   C 'I look dreadful'
   B 'I'm going to work now'   D 'I feel all right now'

3   Doris thought he shouldn't go back to work because
   A he couldn't see the doctor
   B he was too ill
   C he didn't want to work
   D it was too late

4   Ed was sent to Kingston Hospital by
   A the doctor   C his work-mates
   B his mother   D Len

5   When Ed came home from the doctor's, he
   A asked for help
   B sat down and did nothing
   C drove straight to the hospital
   D asked Len to drive him to hospital

6   Ed intended to drive himself to hospital because
   A he's very independent
   B his mother didn't offer to drive
   C Len couldn't drive his car
   D he wanted a word with Len

Exercise 2

Put the following events in the order in which they occur in Doris's account.

1   Ed took ages to get into the house.
2   Ed went to the doctor's.
3   Len took Ed to the hospital.
4   Ed came home from work.
5   The doctor told Ed he would have to go to Kingston Hospital.

6   Len went to talk to Ed.
7   Ed got the car to the garage.
8   Ed came back from the doctor's and sat down.
9   Doris came home from Carol's.
10 The doctor told Ed that he was anaemic.

Exercise 3

Ed was ill, so he went to the doctor. Complete the sentences below in the same pattern saying what Ed did in each case.

1   Ed was tired, so . . .
2   Ed was hungry, so . . .
3   Ed was unwell . . .
4   Ed was cold . . .
5   Ed was hot . . .
6   Ed was in a hurry . . .
7   Ed was thirsty . . .
8   Ed was bored . . .

Exercise 4

Use each of the words and phrases in italics in a sentence of your own. You will find them all on the tape.

1   he came *home from work*
2   he was *shivering*
3   he was *so ill*
4   it *took* him *ages*
5   he looked *dreadful*
6   *as you can imagine*
7   you'll *have to go* to hospital
8   they'll probably *keep* you *in*
9   *luckily*
10 Go and *have a word with* him.

3.3   Graham tells the story of a wet camping holiday.

Graham and Bridget have different views of an ideal holiday. Bridget prefers camping but Graham would rather stay in a luxury hotel. However, Graham doesn't mind camping if the weather is good. Unfortunately, they recently had a camping holiday in bad weather.

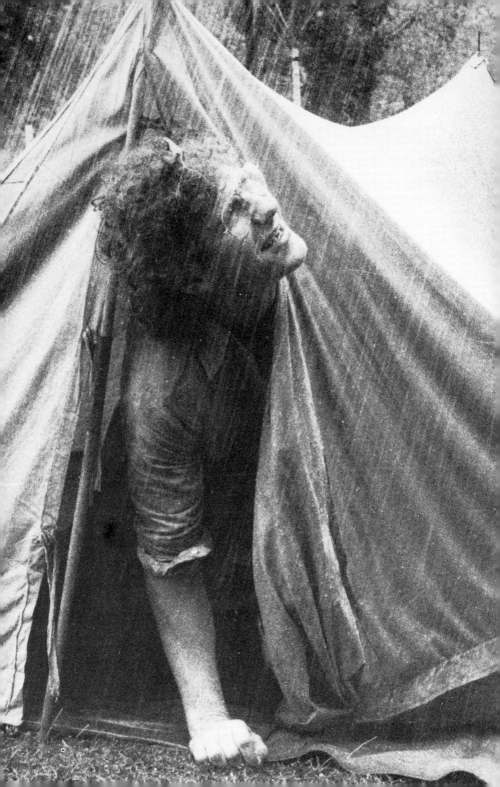

Points of detail

wild Wales — the parts of Wales which are far away from towns and
   people

remote — far away

Yorkshire — a large area of North East England

Lake District — an area in the North West of England, where there
   are beautiful lakes and hills

Skye — an island off the west coast of Scotland

rotten — very bad indeed

get away with — here, tolerate, manage

bearable — tolerable, possible to live in

frozen to death — 'to death' is used to emphasize the adjective
   'frozen'. Another example: 'I've been bitten to death by
   mosquitoes.'

gas burner – a small gas cooker

lull – here, a time when the weather was less unpleasant

Thermos – a special container (a vacuum flask) which keeps the
   contents at the temperature at which you put them in

stew – meat cooked in water, with vegetables etc.

feeling a bit rotten and low — They were feeling unwell and
   unhappy because they hadn't eaten for two days.

an off-peak time – here, a time when not many people are on
   holiday.

the Bahamas — islands in the West Indies

a five-star hotel – a very luxurious hotel

Exercise 1

Give short-form answers to each of the following questions.

1 Is camping Graham's ideal holiday?
2 Does Bridget like the countryside?
3 Does Graham enjoy wet weather holidays?
4 Was the weather good when Graham and Bridget went for
    their recent holiday?
5 Were they living in a tent?
6 Was the wind strong?
7 Could they use their gas burner?
8 Did they eat well?
9 Did the wind drop for a while?
10 Would Graham like another kind of holiday?

Exercise 2

*Find a word or phrase on the tape for which each of the
following words or phrases in italics is an explanation.*

1 *a perfect* holiday

2 we *had very bad luck*
3 *it wasn't only* the wind and rain
4 it was *very cold indeed*
5 we had *two days* when . . .
6 we *succeeded in getting* some soup made
7 the wind *began* again
8 it was a bit *unpleasant*

Exercise 3

*The weather caused a lot of problems for Graham and
Bridget. Complete each of the following sentences,
imagining what the problems would be in each case.*
Example: The wind blew so hard . . .
Answer: The wind blew so hard that they couldn't cook
a meal.

1 It rained so heavily that . . .
2 It was so hot that . . .
3 The ice was so thick that . . .
4 The water was so cold that . . .
5 It was so windy that . . .
6 The sun shone so brightly that . . .
7 The snow was so thick that . . .
8 The rain went on for so long that . . .

Exercise 4

*Bridget likes camping. Graham prefers five-star hotels. List
the good things about each, in your opinion, and then list the
bad things. You should have six to ten points in each of your
four lists.*

Can you say . . .?

Most people like telling stories about things that actually happened to them. Look back at the list at the beginning of the Unit, and, using similar patterns, tell someone about something that happened to you. Try to tell the story so that the listener will know whether you liked what happened or not, whether it worried you or excited you, and so on.

If it's difficult to think of a story, consider the three tapes you've just listened to and think whether anything like that has ever happened to you. Have you ever been delayed on a journey? Have you ever been ill? Have you ever had a holiday ruined by the weather? You will probably say: 'Oh, yes. I remember once when . . .' and your story will begin.

4 People asking for and giving descriptions

4.1 Doris describes what she's going to wear for her son's wedding.

Doris is looking forward to the day when her son will marry Sharon. As the bridegroom's mother, she is anxious to look as smart as possible. She has bought everything she needs and is now telling her friends what she is going to wear. The wedding is to be held in early April, so everyone has a problem deciding whether to wear winter clothes or summer clothes.

Points of detail

walking my shoes in — New shoes are sometimes a bit hard and uncomfortable, so people wear them around the house for an hour or two at a time to make them softer and more comfortable. This is often referred to as 'walking shoes in'.

got all the gear — got all the clothes, etc. 'Gear' is a colloquial word for all the things one wears.

a two-piece — here, a jacket and a skirt

turban hat — a close fitting hat without a brim

to match — to go well with, because it is the same colour

I'd better take my comb with us and comb everybody's hair out — Sharon, the bride, is a hairdresser!

Permission to — Susan uses a formal, military-type expression, meaning 'May I . . .?'

peak hats — hats with a brim which sticks out like a man's cap

If it wasn't that — here, if I wasn't going to be . . .

I wouldn't bother — I wouldn't consider it necessary

Val — i.e. Valerie, Doris's daughter, who will also be going to the wedding

Exercise 1

Answer each of the following questions, using a complete sentence for each answer.

1 Why is Doris walking her shoes in?
2 What colour is the blouse Doris will wear?
3 Does the jacket have short sleeves or long sleeves?
4 Is she going to wear summer clothes or heavy, winter ones?
5 Is Sharon going to do Doris's hair for her before the wedding?
6 Is it necessary to wear a hat for the wedding?
7 What kind of hat has Susan got?
8 Why is a hat necessary for Doris?

Exercise 2

Make a list of the five items of clothing mentioned on the tape. Then add to your list five items of clothing which you might wear in cold weather and five for hot weather.

Exercise 3

For each of the items you have listed in Exercise 2, give a

description which indicates the colour and one other thing about each one.

Example: a long-sleeved, black dress

Exercise 4

Write a brief descriptive paragraph about what, in your view, the fashionable man or woman would wear to go to a wedding in your country.

4.2 Lucy corrects her friends as they try to describe her brother, Matthew.

Avril and Sarah try to give an accurate description of Matthew, but they haven't seen him for some time and Lucy corrects them from time to time. Avril and Sarah don't want to say nasty things about Matthew, but Lucy is able to be much more honest about his appearance.

Points of detail

over six foot — more than six feet tall (approximately two metres)
in proportion with his height — Avril thinks that Matthew is quite thin for somebody of his height.
I would have said — here, it's my opinion
not a bit — not at all
stature — way of standing
upright — straight and tall
slouches — i.e. he stands badly, not upright
two inches shorter — two inches, i.e. five cms, less tall
got a certain quality about him — here, has a special appearance
scruffily — untidily
casual — informal
smart — well dressed, neat
terribly Australian — 'terribly' can be used instead of 'very' to emphasize the adjective that follows, e.g. 'I'm terribly tired. I'll fall asleep in a minute.'
a great effect — a strong influence

Exercise 1

Answer each of the following questions by choosing the right answer from A B C or D.

1 Who does Lucy think can give the best description of Matthew?

  A Avril   C Lucy herself
  B Sarah   D Matthew

2 Matthew looks *very* like

  A Lucy   C his father
  B his mother   D none of them

3 Sarah thinks Matthew is

  A strange   C scruffy
  B tidily casual   D uncomfortable

4 Lucy says this is because

  A her father is smart
  B Matthew has been to Australia
  C Matthew is Australian
  D Matthew is terrible

5 Avril would have believed that Matthew had been in Australia

  A for longer than Lucy says
  B for less time than Lucy says
  C for ever
  D for a very short time

6 Matthew's Australian accent

  A is very noticeable   C isn't noticeable now
  B never was noticeable   D never existed

Exercise 2

Go through the tape carefully and for each part of the description, write down briefly a parallel description of yourself. Begin like this:

'I'm quite tall/short, about (height), and I'm thin/fat/average size. I've got . . .'

Exercise 3

Listen to Exercise 3 on your tape and write down exactly what Sarah says about Matthew.

Exercise 4

Lucy says that Matthew has a big nose. Avril and Sarah don't like to agree, because it's not a very kind thing to say. Write down five more hard descriptive facts which you could use about a person and for each one find a kinder way to say much the same thing.
Example: She's fat.
Possible answer: She's a little larger than average.

4.3   Win and Tom M. describe a miniature caravan.

One day, Win and Tom, who live in the country, went to visit someone who lived in a country cottage. They saw, and were very impressed by, a model caravan which the owner of the cottage had made. It was correct in every detail and worth a lot of money.

Points of detail
renovate — restore, make like new again
miniature — small-scale model
18 inches long — an inch is 25.4 mm
1 foot high — a foot is 30.5 cm
canvas — strong, hard, waterproof cloth
gaudy — very colourful and showy
highly painted — painted in strong colours

Exercise 1

Answer each of the following questions, using a complete sentence for each answer.

1   What is the old man going to do with the old caravan?
2   Is the miniature caravan big enough to get into?
3   How much is the miniature caravan worth?
4   What is the miniature made of?
5   How is it painted?
6   Why did Tom not see very clearly inside the miniature van?

Exercise 2

Write down the opposite to each of the following words and phrases in italics as they are used in the conversation.

1   a *very old* caravan

2 *as much as possible*
3 *very tiny*
4 painted with *all the lines*
5 everything has to be *gaudy*
6 Is it done *inside*?

Exercise 3

*Make a list of things that you have seen in miniature form,
e.g. ships, aeroplanes.*

Can you say . . .?

Have another look at the expressions listed at the beginning
of the Unit. Try to describe someone you can see from
where you're sitting. Decide first of all whether you are
going to be kind in your description or very honest.

Now give a description of something or somewhere else,
e.g.
— a tour
— clothes
— a picture
— a room
— a hair-style
— a holiday resort

---

5 People talking about things they dislike

5.1 Moira and Colin and Mary consider what their pet hates are.

It is day-to-day domestic jobs which Moira and Mary don't like doing. Colin doesn't feel so strongly about these things, perhaps because he doesn't have to do them so often, but he does find that milk bottles are a problem!

Points of detail
my pet hate — the thing I hate doing most
pegging out — putting clothes on the washing-line with pegs
for years and years — for many years
I don't care for — a more gentle way of saying 'I don't like'
off-putting — a colloquialism meaning 'distracting', e.g. 'I can't concentrate on my work. That music is very off-putting.'

irksome — annoying

taking it away downstairs — Colin and Moira live in a flat at the top
   of a house and so they have to carry their kitchen rubbish bin
   downstairs to empty it.

accumulated — gathered, collected

so many journeys — here, journeys from the flat to the front door.
   Milk is delivered daily to each house in Britain and people are
   expected to put their empty milk bottles on the door-step for the
   milkman to take them away next day.

multiply — increase in number

breed like rabbits — i.e. the number of milk bottles increases as fast
   as rabbits reproduce

kitchen counter – a flat surface in the kitchen where food is
   prepared, etc.

Exercise 1

Decide whether each of these statements is true or false.

1 Mary likes hanging out washing more than any other
   household job.
2 Moira didn't like hanging out washing in the summer.
3 Moira dislikes ironing.
4 Moira likes the smell of ironing.
5 Nobody likes the smell of clean, newly ironed clothes.
6 Colin thinks it is difficult to keep pets.
7 Colin likes all household jobs.
8 Someone collects the rubbish directly from Colin's flat.
9 Colin and Moira don't like milk bottles.
10 Colin and Moira breed rabbits.

Exercise 2

*Use each of the following words and phrases in italics in a
sentence of your own to show that you know what it means.*

1 *My pet hate* is . . .
2 *I loathe* pegging out washing
3 *for years and years*
4 it was *nice and hot*
5 that is *very nasty indeed*
6 *I don't care for* ironing
7 I find it very *off-putting*
8 *lots of* little jobs
9 emptying *the rubbish*
10 you've *accumulated* 65 bottles

11   Milk bottles are *pretty* bad
12   They *multiply*

🎧 **Exercise 3**

Listen to Exercise 3 on your tape and write down the groups of three words which you hear. Listen very carefully. You will hear each group of words twice. There are eight groups.

Exercise 4

Make a list of your pet hates using the pattern given in the examples. Even if you only have one or two really pet hates, make a list of at least ten things which you dislike doing.
Examples: emptying the rubbish
              cleaning out the garage
              buying shoes

5.2   Tim C. expresses his dislike of cooking and shopping.

Tim is always willing to help his wife, who, like him, has a full-time job. However, he doesn't like cooking very much and here he explains why that is.

Points of detail
shoddy — poor quality
second-rate — inferior, poor quality
inevitably — without doubt
lack — don't have
a horrifying experience — a frightening thing to do. But Tim is
    exaggerating!

🎧 **Exercise 1**

Answer each of the following questions using a short but complete sentence for each answer.

1   What is Tim's attitude to cooking?
2   What reason does he give for this attitude?
3   Is he good at shopping?
4   What does he think of the prices of goods in the shops?
5   What does Tim lack when he starts cooking?
6   How long can Tim stay in the supermarket without feeling he
     must leave?

43

🎧 **Exercise 2**

Listen to Exercise 2 on your tape and write down exactly what Tim says.

Exercise 3

Make a shopping list in four parts. You can plan to spend as much money as you like!

1 Things you need to prepare a meal.
2 Things you need for the house.
3 Things you need for the car.
4 Presents you need to buy for four people.

5.3 Frank talks about his dislike of the sea and beaches.

Frank and Liz have considerable differences of opinion about the sea. Liz is a very keen swimmer, but Frank doesn't like water at all. Here he tells Mary what it is that he doesn't like about being at the sea-side.

Points of detail
partly — here, this is part of the reason
a waste of energy — using energy for no useful purpose
salty — tasting of salt
pebbles — small round stones, found on beaches
generally — here, in most cases; not the meaning associated with
    time as in 'Generally, he comes at five' — meaning 'usually'
a bone of contention — an idiom meaning 'a subject of argument'
sitting about — implies sitting doing nothing
caked — 'to cake' is usually used with something more sticky than
    salt, e.g. 'caked with mud', but here Frank means that he feels
    covered with a coat of salt
such a tradition — a custom, a long history of members of the family
    doing the same things as their fathers and grandfathers did
for ease and elegance — i.e. he swam in a relaxed and graceful way
the baths — the swimming-pool

🎧 **Exercise 1**

List all the things that Frank says he doesn't like about the sea-side. You should find five or six.

45

Exercise 2

Use each of the following phrases in italics in a sentence of your own to show that you have understood the meaning.

1 *it seems to me*
2 *a waste* of energy
3 *salty* water
4 on the *pebbles*
5 I don't like *sitting about*
6 *going in the water*
7 your hair *full of* salt
8 *doing nothing*
9 *it's very strange*
10 such a *tradition*

Exercise 3

Frank doesn't like swimming. He doesn't like beaches. List eight things he might enjoy doing at the sea-side that would probably not be possible to do at home.

Can you say . . .?

Now go back to the list at the beginning of the Unit. Try to use some of the expressions you find there in talking about things you dislike. For some things take the view that you simply don't like this or that, but for others be stronger in your dislike, and use expressions like 'I hate . . .' and 'I loathe . . .' Choose topics from this list if you wish:
    — travelling in aeroplanes/ships/cars/etc.
    — working in a particular place
    — your neighbours
    — crowds
    — shopping

---

6 People asking for and giving advice

> **They say . . .**
>
> What sort of clothes?
> I think you can wear anything
> Then you can wear . . .
> It would look . . .
> Long skirts are still all right, are they?
> I think they're very much in
>
> You can, of course, make certain things . . .
> You could buy some . . .
> Can you think of some simple things?
> You might like to try . . .
> You think sandwiches are a good idea?
> What shall I put . . .
> Ham would be fine
> You wouldn't go for salami
> Easy to make . . .
> That would be a good one
> Put it through a mincer
> Do you think I ought to . . .?
> It's a good idea to . . .
>
> Well, if you . . .
> You might try going to . . .
> There are agencies who are . . .
> Unskilled clerical work is available
> You can get . . .

6.1 Mary asks her friends for advice about what to wear on holiday.

Mary wants advice about the sort of clothes to wear in a hotel in the evening when she goes on holiday. Scilla and Celia have a number of ideas and Felix contributes by reporting what his wife wears on such occasions.

Points of detail

these days — at the present time

top — garment which is worn above the waist, e.g. a blouse, a
  sweater, a shirt, etc.

down to here — Scilla points to her arm as she speaks, showing
  that by 'down to here' she means down to the elbow or a little
  shorter.

waistcoat — short, sleeveless jacket

tunic-top — Celia describes this garment later in the conversation

jacket-type — like a jacket

polo-neck — a high collar which is turned down at the neck

tight-fitting — close to the body, not loose

slinky — here, smooth, like a snake skin

young things — young people

somewhat — rather

they're very much in — i.e. in fashion

a multitude of sins — a large number of faults

Exercise 1

*Answer each of the following questions by choosing the
right answer from A B C or D.*

1 Mary wants advice on
   A women in hotels
   B where to have dinner in a hotel
   C what to wear for dinner in a hotel
   D what to eat for dinner

2 Which of the following does Felix *not* mention?
   A a blouse under a jumper   C a thin blouse on its own
   B a jumper under a blouse   D a long skirt

3 Scilla recommends a 'top' which
   A is loose   C is a waistcoat
   B ruins your hair   D has buttons

4 Scilla and Celia give ideas about what to wear underneath
   the top. Which of the following do they *not* mention?
   A a polo-neck sweater   C a shirt
   B a sweater without sleeves D nothing at all

5 Scilla believes that if you are not young, you should
   A wear something under the tunic
   B wear nothing under the tunic
   C not wear a tunic at all
   D never wear anything but a tunic

48

6   Celia tells Mary that long skirts are
     A not very fashionable
     B not right at all
     C very fashionable
     D very sinful

Exercise 2

For each of the following words and phrases in italics find another word of similar meaning.

1   . . . women wear *these days*
2   *how warm* it is
3   a *thin* blouse
4   a *jumper*
5   *instead of* having a waistcoat
6   *ruins* your hair
7   *if you wish*
8   cover yourself up *a bit*
9   long skirts are *all right*
10   a *multitude* of sins

Exercise 3

Make a list of ten things that are 'in' in your country at the present time. They don't have to be clothes; breakfast parties may be the 'in' thing, or perhaps slimming is 'in'.

6.2   Ray gives advice on what food to prepare for a children's party.

As a professional cook, Ray has lots of ideas for feeding young children. His wife, Isabel, is less happy about the task, so she asks Ray to give her some advice. She is anxious not to have too much work in preparing the food, as she doesn't expect to have much time to spare.

Points of detail
jellies — a sweet dish made with water and fruit-flavoured gelatine
ripple ice-cream — a block of ice-cream with wavy lines of a fruit
    sauce running through it so that the sauce looks like ripples on
    water

sponge-cake — light cake made with eggs, sugar and flour
icing — sugar mixture, made by adding the white of an egg to fine
    icing-sugar, used to decorate cakes
blancmanges — flavoured milk puddings, eaten cold
wouldn't go for — wouldn't choose
salami — an Italian sausage, salted and flavoured with garlic
palate — here, sense of taste
mince up — cut into very small pieces
a mincer — a machine used for mincing
mayonnaise — a creamy sauce used on salads or cold meat
a grater — a kitchen tool used to rub food into quite small pieces,
    but not as small as a mincer does
cases — containers
pastry cases — shapes made with pastry

Exercise 1

*Decide which of the following is true and which is false,
according to the tape.*

1 Ray doesn't recommend coloured ice-creams.
2 Ray would put jelly with sponge cake.
3 He suggests cutting the cake into small pieces.
4 He thinks sandwiches would be useful.
5 Isabel has already decided what to put in the sandwiches.
6 Ray thinks children would like salami.
7 Chicken would be too strong for children.
8 Ray is the first to mention egg sandwiches.
9 Making a cake would be no trouble.
10 Pastry cases would be useful to put the cake pieces into.

Exercise 2

*Find a word or phrase opposite in meaning to each of the
words and phrases in italics. They are all taken from the tape.*

1 very, very *simple*
2 *small* individual jellies
3 *differences* of colour
4 you could *buy*
5 *a lot of* work
6 a *good* idea
7 chicken is rather *nice*

🎧 **Exercise 3**

Listen to Exercise 3 on your tape and fill in the blanks below.

'You can, ..., make certain things . . . . which
would be very, very . . . . to do. You could make very,
small ·. . . . . jellies, different . . . . jellies; you
could . . . . some ripple . . . . or a . . . . of
coloured ice-creams and put small . . . . of ice-cream
with the . . . ., but again emphasis being on . . . .
of . . . .'

Exercise 4

*Imagine that you are going to entertain four very old people
and want to give them supper. Make a list of food suitable
for old people to eat in the evening.*

6.3 Susan asks for advice about getting a temporary job.

As a full-time student, Susan finds that she has time to get a
job, to earn a little money, during the Christmas vacation.
She is not sure about how to find a job for such a short time
and she asks Felix and Scilla for advice.

Points of detail

type — use a typewriter

shorthand — an abbreviated kind of writing used by secretaries
when they take dictation

secretarial stuff — Susan means that she can't do a secretarial kind
of job.

Yeah — a casual (slang) way of saying 'Yes'

a week or so — a week or a little more. 'or so' is used quite
frequently in this way, e.g. 'I can lend you a pound or so, if that
helps'; 'You'll have to wait an hour or so.'

agencies — here, employment agencies, where those looking for
work can find out about possible employers and vice versa

temp/temporary — for a short time only

department store — a very large shop, with a lot of departments
selling a wide variety of goods

telephonists — people who operate telephones. Notice that the
stress changes: 'telephone, tel'ephonist

counter clerks — people who work in shops, offices, etc, meeting
people who come to buy goods or seek services

unskilled — without expertise or training

clerical work — work as a clerk

over this period — during this time

a washer-up — a person who washes the dishes. Felix invents the word from the verb 'to wash up'

jobs going — jobs available

Boxing Day — the day after Christmas Day

Exercise 1

Answer the following questions, using a complete sentence for each answer.

1 What does Susan say she can't do?
2 For how long does she want to work?
3 Where does Scilla say Susan should go to try to get a temporary job?
4 Does Scilla think it will be easy to get a job?
5 Why does Felix think a department store needs extra staff at this time of year?
6 Does Scilla think Susan will get a job in a department store?
7 What sort of workers are agencies looking for?
8 Is Susan willing to be a waitress?

Exercise 2

List all the jobs mentioned by Felix and Scilla as they try to advise Susan. You should find six. Add to your list six other jobs which Susan might be able to do on a temporary basis.

Exercise 3

Find the words and phrases from the conversation for which each of the following words and phrases in italics is an explanation.

1 What sort of job are you *seeking*?
2 Anything I'm *able to do*
3 a job just *for a short time*
4 *short-term* jobs
5 find something *without any difficulty*
6 But *definitely* there are agencies . . .
7 *untrained* clerical work
8 In restaurants, as well, *at this time*
9 *willing* to work

53

Exercise 4

There are many jobs which are seasonal, i.e. they are only done at certain times of year, e.g. grape harvesting in France in September or October, strawberry picking in England in June. Make a list of at least eight seasonal jobs, not forgetting to put the place where it is done because the seasons vary from country to country.

Can you say . . .?

The list at the beginning of the Unit will help you to ask for and to give advice. Take some of the topics below, or others if you prefer, and seek advice from your friends or give them advice.
— about English classes
— about how to behave in a certain country
— about clothes for a man (for sports, a disco, etc.)
— about improving your appearance
— about getting a mark off a coat
— about sightseeing in your area
— about a family argument

7 People asking for and giving reasons

<table>
<tr><td>

They say . . .

Why do you think they work?
Why do they work?
I think . . . because . . .
This was so that you could say . . .
This was because . . .
Ah, so it was . . .?
Well, I put it down to . . .

Why not?
I think they should . . .
Why?
It's not wrong because you're charged a rate.
No, because they depend on the tips.

Why did you sell the car?
Because it had conked out . . .
Why did you choose that particular car?
A number of reasons: one, it's . . .
The main reason is because . . .
Because you like the look of it
Because that would be the reason why I would . . .

</td></tr>
</table>

7.1 Beryl gives reasons why a Slimming Club is successful.

Tim and Beryl have been considering the problems of overweight and underweight people. When she says that she learned something about these problems at a Slimming Club, Tim is interested to know why these clubs are successful.

Points of detail
expertise — knowledge
lies — here, comes from

attendance — here, going to

the course — the programme of meetings

target weight — the weight which you wish to reach

they work — here, 'work' means 'operate successfully, properly', e.g.
'I can't use this bicycle. The brakes don't work.'

group dynamics — the reactions of individuals in a group to each
other

the mechanism — here, the way of operating, the method

induces — brings about, causes

camaraderie — friendliness, a feeling of all being in the same
situation. Beryl actually says 'camaradie'.

give things up — here, stop eating things

I must confess — I must admit

in my case — for me

competitive — wishing to win, to do better than the others

stuck to — kept to, continued, persevered with

diet — eating plan

smug superiority — self-satisfied feeling of being the best

put it down as — normally one would say 'put it down to', meaning
'say it was caused by'

Exercise 1

Answer each of the following questions very briefly.

1 Where did Beryl learn about weight problems?
2 How often has she joined a Slimming Club?
3 How often has she completed the course?
4 What has usually prevented her from completing the course?
5 Does Beryl believe in Slimming Clubs?
6 How many men has Beryl met at Slimming Clubs?
7 When was the last time Beryl went to a Slimming Club?
8 For how long did she go on with her diet on that occasion?
9 For how long should she have gone on?
10 Who was the most successful slimmer at the Club?

Exercise 2

*Use each of the following words and phrases in italics in a
sentence of your own to show that you understand what it
means.*

1 my *expertise*
2 on two *occasions*
3 I've never *completed. . .*
4 *for one reason or another*
5 *of any real value*

56

6   Why do they *work?*
7   they *rely on* group dynamics
8   *suffering*
9   *lose weight*
10 I must *confess*
11 I stuck to my *diet*
12 *by* the next Friday

Exercise 3

List at least ten things that you might do to lose weight.

Exercise 4

Now complete the excuses below by adding a reason to each one.

1   I'm overweight because . . .
2   I was late today . . .
3   I would have been earlier but . . .
4   It wasn't my fault but . . .
5   I haven't got my homework . . .
6   Your car isn't finished . . .
7   The post is late . . .
8   I can't marry you . . .
9   I'm wet through . . .
10 I can't pay . . .

7.2 Tim C. and Beryl justify their unwillingness to give tips.

Mary is amazed that Beryl doesn't give a tip to the hairdresser, but both Beryl and Tim feel that they are perfectly justified in not giving tips. They believe that the system of payment is wrong and that tipping should not be necessary.

Points of detail
tip — give a small extra sum of money to someone who has given you good service
the going rate — the proper amount of money
subsidize — give additional payments to
patronizing — treating someone as an inferior
I wouldn't bet on it — I wouldn't be so certain about it .
at times — sometimes

if, say — 'say' is used in this way to mean 'for example', e.g. 'Are you generous?' 'What do you mean?' 'Well, if, say, I asked you for £100 . . .'
a rate — a fixed price
to make their living — to live on, to pay their everyday expenses
depend on — rely on; here, expect the tips as part of their income
how much the market will stand — here, how much people using taxis are willing to pay

Exercise 1

Say whether each of the statements below is true or false, according to the conversation you have just listened to.

1 Mary is surprised that Beryl doesn't tip the hairdresser.
2 Beryl never tips a hairdresser.
3 Beryl thinks the young girls should be paid more.
4 Because she doesn't tip, Beryl gets her hair done more cheaply than other people.
5 Other people pay for Beryl to have her hair done.
6 Tim likes giving tips.
7 Mary expects everyone to give tips.
8 Tim thinks taxi fares are high.
9 Tim gives taxi-drivers big tips.
10 Taxi-drivers, according to Tim, should know what their work is worth.

Exercise 2

Make all the positive phrases and sentences below negative and all the negative ones, positive.

1 They should pay the girls . . .
2 I get my hair done at a lower price.
3 They subsidize me.
4 I don't like that.
5 You can't *not* tip.
6 I'll give them the rest of the change.
7 If it comes to £1.25 . . .
8 You're charged a rate.

Choose the definition which best fits the words or phrases in italics as they are used on the tape.

1 *Normally*, I do not tip a hairdresser.
   frequently   always
   usually   without end

2 They should *not expect* the customers to subsidize it.
   not want   not hope
   not rely on   not wait for

3 What *happens*, of course, is . . .
   occurs   chances
   waits   expects

4 I *dislike* the whole idea of tips.
   despise   don't like
   disown   don't recognize

5 I wouldn't *bet on it*.
   not expect it   pay for it
   expect it   put money on it

6 *Particularly* with the cost of taxis now.
   at present   especially
   in practice   practically

7 You're *charged a rate*.
   asked to pay a certain price
   asked to pay too much
   expected to pay more than you're asked
   asked to pay what you can

8 They've obviously *calculated the amount* . . .
   lost the money   asked for the money
   worked out the price   paid the price

Exercise 4

Tipping is not allowed at all in some countries and the services we tip for vary from country to country. If you could give a tip to just five people in a year, who would you choose and why? Write sentences like the one in the example.
Example: I would tip my dustman because he does a job
          which is dirty and unpopular.

7.3 Felix explains why he has bought a new car.

Felix has just bought a new car and he tells his friends why
he sold his old car and why he likes his new car. He has
obviously thought a lot about both the old car and the new
one, as he lists a large number of points about each of them.

Points of detail
giving me trouble — causing me problems
both ways — here, both by trying to get the old car repaired and by
    eventually selling it and buying a new one
on its last legs — at the end of its useful life, e.g. 'We'll have to buy
    a new television set. This one is on its last legs.'
had a lot needed doing to it — had a lot of things which needed
    repairing
it had conked out on me — it had broken down, something had
    gone wrong when I was trying to use it
set off — start a journey
listening out — listening carefully, e.g. 'I'm just going next door.
    Please listen out for the baby crying.'
second-hand — i.e. it belonged to somebody else before
Triumph Dolomite — a British car
compact — neat
sporty-saloon — a family car, but one which looks rather like a
    sports car
four full seats — i.e. four full-sized seats

Exercise 1

*Answer each of the following questions by choosing the
most appropriate answer from A B C or D.*

1 Felix sold his old car because
  A he had too much money
  B he needed money
  C the car was breaking down too often
  D the car wouldn't go at all

2 Felix felt that his old car
  A wouldn't last long
  B would go on forever
  C would be all right for a number of years
  D was of no use to anybody

3 The new car
   A never gets to the other end of a journey
   B should never be used at the other end of a journey
   C should get to the other end of a journey
   D shouldn't be used for long journeys

4 The old car had broken down
   A once   C never
   B a few times   D frequently

5 The main reason why Felix chose a Triumph Dolomite was
   because
   A it looks nice   C it's comfortable
   B it's a fast car   D it's a sports car

6 Scilla is surprised that a man should buy a particular car
   because it looks nice. In her opinion,
   A it's not important
   B that's a typically male reason for buying a car
   C that's a typically female reason for buying a car
   D that car doesn't look nice

Exercise 2

List all the points of complaint which Felix makes about his old car and then list all the good points about the new car.

Exercise 3

Listen to Exercise 3 on your tape and write down exactly what Felix says.

Exercise 4

You must own something that you would like to replace — a watch? a radio? a bed? a house? Write down all the reasons you can think of for getting rid of the old one, and what good things you would find in a new one.
Examples: I'd like a new watch because this old one . . .
It would be nice to have a new one because it . . .

Can you say . . .?

The expressions listed at the beginning of the Unit will be useful now, but note that people often give reasons without using 'because' and 'so that' and so on. To practise, answer some of the questions below with 'Yes' or 'No' and then add your reasons.

Do you give tips? Why? Why not?

Do you think a Slimming Club is a good idea? Why? Why not?

Do you think large families are happier than small ones? Why? Why not?

Do you wish you were more clever than you are? Why? Why not?

Do you wish you were famous? Why? Why not?

Do you wish you were rich? Why? Why not?

8 People telling others how to do something

They say . . .

Go to the top of this road
Turn left
Then go straight ahead
Turn right
Go all the way down . . .
Stop
You go along to . . .

I do suggest, in that case, that you get . . .
Put the eggs and sugar in the bowl
Whisk them
That's important, that you . . .
Pour the mixture
Place in an oven
Try not to disturb it

The first thing is to . . .
You need to sandpaper down the woodwork
The first rule is, spend . . .
Get things like Elastoplast
Do it and do it well
Fill in cracks
Sandpaper down

8.1 Tom J. tells Simon how to get to his house.

Simon intends to go to Tom's house for the first time. He wants to go there by car. Tom tells him which way to go. Notice how Tom speaks more and more quickly because to him the way is very familiar. Simon will clearly need to make some notes if he is to find his way!

Points of detail

ahead — forward

a T-junction — a place on a road where it is only possible to go
either left or right

Richmond Hill — a well-known hill on the outskirts of London,
from which there is a beautiful view of the Thames

one-way — a street where traffic is only allowed to travel in one
direction

Nightingale Lane — a lane is a small, country road. A nightingale is
a small bird which sings at night.

Richmond Bridge — a bridge over the River Thames

Exercise 1

*Answer each of the following questions using a complete
sentence for each answer.*

1 Where is Simon to turn left for the first time?
2 What is the first instruction Tom gives Simon about what to
do when he gets to the T-junction?
3 Why is there a problem about this instruction?
4 What does Tom think of the name Nightingale Lane?
5 How far down Nightingale Lane is Simon to go?
6 What must Simon do at the traffic lights?
7 How will he cross the river?
8 What must he do at the next traffic lights?
9 How far are these lights after the bridge?
10 Does Simon think he'll remember the directions?

Exercise 2

Write down instructions for

1 getting from where you're sitting to your house
2 from your house to the centre of town
3 from your house to the nearest library, swimming pool or
post office

Exercise 3

*Listen to Exercise 3 on your tape and write down each group
of three words. Underline the word in each group which you
have heard in Tom's directions. You will hear each group
twice. There are ten groups.*

8.2 Ray tells one of his neighbours how to make a cake.

Julia, one of Ray's neighbours, knows that Ray is an expert cook. She wants to make a specially light sponge cake and so she asks Ray to give her some instructions.

Points of detail
delicate, feather-light — fine, light in texture
sponge — a light cake made with eggs, sugar and flour
a whisk — a kitchen tool with which to beat eggs to make them
    light and full of air
a bowl — a deep dish
formula — here, method
ounces — 16 ounces make one pound. One ounce = 28.35 grams.
doubled, tripled, quadrupled — become twice, three times, four
    times greater in quantity
fluffy — soft and light
dribbling it — letting it fall a little at a time
at that point — at that moment, at that time
fold in — here, to stir in gently with a spoon
buttered and floured — i.e. rubbed with butter and sprinkled with
    flour
flan-case — flat dish
375°–400° Fahrenheit = approx. 190°–260° Centigrade
draughts — movements of air in a room or other enclosed place
gas mark — Gas ovens usually have controls marked with numbers
    from 1 to 9, to indicate various temperatures.

Exercise 1

Answer each of the following questions by choosing the most appropriate answer from A B C or D, according to the conversation.

1 Julia will make the sponge by hand because
    A she hasn't got a machine
    B she prefers to do it by hand
    C Ray tells her to do it by hand
    D her machine isn't working

2 Julia must start by putting
    A the flour in the bowl
    B the whisk in the bowl
    C the eggs and sugar in the bowl
    D the eggs and sugar and flour in the bowl

3 Ray tells her to whisk the eggs and sugar
  A for a long time   C for a moment or two
  B in hot water   D until the eggs separate

4 The flour must be
  A whisked a lot in the mixture
  B added gently to the mixture
  C whisked with the eggs
  D not mixed in at all

5 When the mixture is ready, Julia must put it
  A in water   C in flour
  B in a dish   D in butter

6 The cake must be cooked
  A in a cool oven for 20 minutes
  B in a draught
  C in a hot oven for 7 minutes
  D in a hot oven for 20 minutes

Exercise 2

Find the word or phrase on the tape for which each of the following words or phrases in italics is an explanation.

1 it's not really *very hard*
2 I do *propose*
3 use the 3-3-3 *method*
4 and *beat* them over some heat
5 until they've *increased*
6 *at that moment* it would be ready
7 *not roughly*
8 *put* the mixture
9 you've buttered *earlier*
10 try not to *move* it

Exercise 3

In each of the groups of words below, underline the things that you might use for each of the activities.
Example: to make a cake — <u>whisk</u>, <u>oven</u>, spade, <u>bowl</u>

1 to clean a room — duster, tyre, polish, fork, brush
2 to write a book – paper, pen, water, ball, duster
3 to make a table — wood, saw, hammer, fork, shorts

4 to lay a table — knives, clothes, spoons, glasses, sandpaper
5 to knit a sweater — spanner, needles, wool, pattern, string
6 to repair a car — spanner, envelope, goal-posts, wallpaper, screwdriver
7 to take a photo — duster, camera, water, screwdriver, film
8 to send a letter — paper, envelope, string, stamp, post-box
9 to decorate a room — wallpaper, paint, cheese, sandpaper, file, paper
10 to play football — ball, shorts, hammer, goal-posts, cheese

Exercise 4

Imagine that a friend has asked you for a new idea for a meal. Think of something you can cook and write down instructions for making it and cooking it as you would write it to send to him/her by post.

8.3 Liz and Frank tell Sarah how to set about decorating a room.

Sarah has decided to try to decorate her bedroom herself. She has never done any decorating before. Liz and Frank have a lot of experience and so they give her some guidance on how to start.

Points of detail

sandpaper — a specially made rough paper with which to smooth walls and woodwork (i.e. doors, window-frames, etc.)
paint-stripper — a chemical preparation which removes paint
like mad — a lot, e.g. 'I've been working like mad for these exams.'
rule number one — the first important thing that must be done
pessimistic estimates — here, most depressing calculations about how long it will take
God! — here used as an exclamation of amazement
it pays, it pays off — it is worthwhile, e.g. 'It pays to study before exams.'
Elastoplast — the trade name of a particular kind of sticking plaster, used to cover and protect small cuts, etc.
Polyfilla — the trade-name of a kind of material which can be used to fill cracks in walls, etc.
you can't go wrong — you can't make a mistake

⌕ Exercise 1

Listen carefully to what Liz and Frank say and decide which of the following statements is true and which is false.

1 Sandpaper is useful for the home decorator.
2 Sandpaper cannot be used on woodwork.
3 Wallpaper always has to be removed.
4 Greasy finger-marks should be washed off.
5 Frank and Liz don't think it worthwhile spending time on sandpapering.
6 Preparing a room for decoration takes less time than one expects.
7 Elastoplast is useful to stick over cracks in the walls.
8 A well prepared surface is wrong.

⌕ Exercise 2

Liz and Frank use a lot of specialized words. Write down all the words and phrases which are particularly associated with home decorating. You should find about eight.

🎧 Exercise 3

Listen to Exercise 3 on your tape and write down exactly what Liz says.

Can you say . . .?

Turn back to the list of expressions at the beginning of the Unit. You will notice that many of them use the imperative form of the verb: 'Go up . . .', 'Do it . . .' Another way of instructing or directing is to say: 'You go up . . .', 'You do it . . .'. Using these kinds of expression, give instructions or directions to somebody else about any of these topics:
— gardening
— riding a bicycle or a horse
— driving a car
— where to find something
— where to hide something
— how to speak to somebody

---

9 People talking about advantages and disadvantages

They say ...

From that point of view, it's quite good ...
We have to ... but, on the other hand, we ...
The rooms are so big
If we moved to a house, we'd find that the rooms were
   much smaller
We've got lots and lots of windows, which means we have
   to wash lots of curtains
It's nice because ...
It's such a nuisance having to ...
It's very difficult to ...
It's good for you, isn't it?

There's far too much traffic
It's a lovely cycle
But the danger is ...
You've got no protection
You don't see them

If you're very tall, I suppose you're always hitting your
   head
You suffer
It's very good at parties
It must be awful being really short

9.1 Avril tells her friends about the good and bad features of the flat she lives in.

Sarah, Lucy and Avril are discussing the places where they
live. Avril explains the advantages and disadvantages of her
home, which is a flat near the top of a block in London. She
obviously likes the flat, although she is realistic enough to
recognize that it has some features which are a nuisance.

Points of detail

we don't get that — Avril means that they don't get noise and dirt in
their third-floor flat

central heating — method of heating a building where all rooms are
warmed from a central heater

switch the fires on — put the fires on

to regulate — to put the temperature at the level you want it

fan heater — a fire with a fan which moves the hot air around the
room

Granny — grandmother, sometimes also called 'Grandma'

a spare room — an extra room for visitors

🎧 Exercise 1

*List all the good and bad features of the flat which Avril
mentions. Put the points under two headings: advantages
and disadvantages.*

🎧 Exercise 2

*Choose the definition which best fits the words and phrases
in italics as they are used in the conversation.*

1   you've got nobody *jumping about* on top
    leaping downstairs   moving noisily
    making a noise   attacking

2   there are advantages and *disadvantages*
    complications   snags
    alterations   disappointments

3   *simply* because they were nearer the street
    merely   plainly
    in a simple way   justifiably

4   they were *nearer* the street
    opposite   closer
    approximately   touching

5   they were nearer *the street*
    the path   the road
    the lane   the pavement

6   we've got *lots and lots* of windows
    more than enough   a large number
    enough   too many

7   *it's nice* because you get a lot of light
    it's pretty   it's neat
    it's good   it's light

8   complain about the *lack* of central heating
    absence   non-appearance
    shortage   weakness

9   *make sure* all the fires are switched off
    look to see   be certain
    ask someone   forget to look

10 it's difficult to *regulate*
    check   switch off
    switch on   control

Exercise 3

*Complete each of the following sentences by adding first an
advantage and then a disadvantage.*
Example: The house is . . . but . . .
Possible answer: The house is large but it hasn't got central
                  heating.

1   The car is . . . but . . .
2   The dog is . . . but . . .
3   Our teacher is . . . but . . .
4   My parents are . . . but . . .
5   Being a pop-star is . . . but . . .
6   Living here is . . . but . . .
7   Working on Saturdays is . . . but . . .
8   Studying English is . . . but . . .

9.2   Frank and Liz consider the advantages and disadvantages of cycling.

Mary asks Frank and Liz whether they would cycle — to
work or for pleasure — because she knows that they live just
outside the gate of Richmond Park (London's largest park)
and cycling is allowed in the park. Frank and Liz are not
enthusiastic as they believe that the disadvantages outweigh
the advantages.

Points of detail
a lovely cycle — i.e. a lovely cycle ride

73

Kingston — a town to the west of London
get through — here, ride through
Richmond — a town near Kingston, and about ten miles from
   Central London
traffic is very heavy — i.e. there is a lot of traffic in Richmond
sceptical — here, inclined not to
invisible — Liz means that it is easy for a car driver to fail to see a
   bicycle.

⏻ Exercise 1

Decide whether each of these statements is true or false,
according to what Frank and Liz say.

1 Cycling is dangerous.
2 There isn't much traffic on the roads.
3 Liz and Frank have often discussed whether to cycle.
4 It's lovely to cycle through the park.
5 If you cycle through the park, you must go through Kingston
   too.
6 Richmond is quiet.
7 Car-drivers often fail to see cyclists.
8 Liz would cycle.
9 Liz needs to cycle.
10 Liz would rather walk at the week-ends.

⏻ Exercise 2

For each of the following words and phrases in italics, find a
word or phrase opposite in meaning.

1 Is it *dangerous*?
2 because of the *danger*
3 *far too much* traffic
4 We *often* discuss it
5 it's a *lovely* cycle
6 *the whole of* the big town
7 traffic is *very heavy*
8 *how quickly* bicycles are . . .
9 *invisible* when they're beside . . .
10 walk *at the week-end*

🎧 Exercise 3

Listen to Exercise 3 on your tape and write down exactly
what Frank says.

Exercise 4

Complete each of the following sentences by adding an advantage.

Example: Riding a bicycle is dangerous but it's a cheap way
to travel.

1 Living at the top of a high block of flats is dangerous but . . .
2 Drinking alcohol is dangerous but . . .
3 Taking drugs is dangerous but . . .
4 Smoking is dangerous but . . .
5 Eating too much is dangerous but . . .
6 Ski-ing is dangerous but . . .
7 Flying is dangerous but . . .
8 Riding a horse is dangerous but . . .
9 Sailing is dangerous but . . .
10 Mountaineering is dangerous but . . .

**9.3 Tom J., Simon, Susan and Sarah look at the
advantages and disadvantages of being tall or
being short.**

Tom and Sarah are both of average height, but Simon is a
rather tall person and speaks from experience. He knows
first-hand the problems of being taller than most other
people. When they come to shortness, none of them has
such clear ideas.

Points of detail
back-ache — pain in the back. Other examples: tooth-ache, head-
ache, neck-ache, etc.
washing-up — washing the dishes
slide down — move smoothly down
tap — touch
making rude noises — here, complaining
drag on the floor — brush along the floor

Exercise 1

*Answer each of the following questions using a complete
sentence for each answer.*

1 What sort of people hit their heads on door-ways and lights?
2 What causes tall people to get back-ache?
3 Why do tall people have to slide down into their seats in the
cinema?

4 Why does Susan think it's an advantage to be tall at Christmas?
5 Why is it useful to be tall at parties?
6 Would Tom rather be tall or short?
7 How does Sarah try to define 'short' in answer to Tom's question 'How short do we really mean by short?'

Exercise 2

Find a word or phrase on the tape for which each of the following is an explanation.

1 *banging* your head
2 you suffer from *continual* back-ache
3 someone will *touch* you on the shoulder
4 *not at ease* when you go into a cinema
5 *all the people* behind you
6 *impolite* noises
7 you can *put* things *up* on the ceiling
8 somebody who's very *uninteresting*
9 you want to *escape from* them
10 it must be *horrible* being really short

Exercise 3

List some light-hearted advantages and disadvantages of being very fat or very thin. Put at least five points on each of your four lists.

Can you say . . .?

Going back to the list at the beginning of this Unit will be of some help to you, but it is *how* things are said as much as *what* is said which indicates that you are stating advantages and disadvantages. Bearing this in mind, try to convey to someone else what you think are the 'pros and cons' (the advantages and disadvantages) of some of the following:
— modern medicine
— modern housing
— modern forms of travel
— compulsory education
— paying taxes

10 People remembering the past

They say . . .

Nigel wasn't too keen
I went along as well
We had the time of our lives
There were all these girls there
We'd never seen girls before
We used to cycle down after school
We always cycled to school
What was it?
We got up with these . . .
Did you learn any ballroom dancing?

I remember being in a high-chair
That's what happened
Where was that?
I must have been about two
My sister was born in Jersey
Where were you born?
My parents lived . . .
Times were quite hard
I used to be . . .

Do you remember falling in love?
I can remember the first time I met you
By the next day . . .
I remember when I first saw Isabel
I'll never forget that really
You must have been quite young
Sixteen, I was, then

10.1 Graham and Nigel remember the time when they learned to dance.

Nigel and Graham have been friends since their schooldays.

They often look back on those days when they enjoyed so many adventures together. Here, they talk about the time when, as teenagers, they started to go to ballroom dancing classes, which they found great fun.

Points of detail

the third year — i.e. the third year in secondary school, when they were about thirteen or fourteen years old

ballroom dancing — a style of dancing which was particularly popular in England in the 1940s and 50s — the waltz, the foxtrot, the quick-step, etc.

Rosalie Morris — the name of the dancing teacher

wasn't too keen on it — didn't like it very much

moral support — here, to keep Nigel company, because there were very few boys in the class

had the time of our lives — enjoyed ourselves very much indeed

we'd troop out — slang for 'we'd go out'

all dressed up to the nines — an idiom meaning 'wearing elaborate and extravagant clothes'

corduroy — a type of cloth, made of thick cotton material with raised lines on it

The Residents' Garden — the name of the place where the classes were held

blokes — slang for 'men'

got up — here, got up to dance

in the 6th form — in the final year at secondary school, aged about seventeen or eighteen

got us into — i.e. got us into the habit of

pub — abbreviation for 'public house', a place where adults (over eighteen) can buy and drink alcoholic drinks

bikes — colloquial and common abbreviation for 'bicycles'

wheel them — push them, rather than ride them

nip — go quickly, e.g. 'It's raining. I'll just nip home and get an umbrella.'

a quick half — a half a pint of beer which they would drink quickly

smelt our breath — i.e. realized that their breath smelt of beer

kid you — 'to kid' is to deceive someone in a light-hearted way, e.g. 'I've bought a super new sports car.' 'Stop kidding! You couldn't even afford a bicycle.'

highly commended — a grade of pass in an examination

bronze medal — an award for passing an examination

Latin American — a style of ballroom dancing, which includes the tango, the cha-cha, etc.

grace — ease of movement

Exercise 1

Give very brief answers to each of the following questions.

1 What year was Nigel in at school when he first went to ballroom dancing lessons?
2 Who was it who knew the dancing teacher?
3 Did Nigel enjoy the first class?
4 How did Nigel and Graham go to school?
5 Where would they have tea before going to the ballroom dancing class?
6 What time did they have to go out to go to the class?
7 What did they wear?
8 Were there more girls or boys at the dancing class?
9 Who persuaded Nigel and Graham to go to the pub after the classes?
10 What did the boys drink?
11 How might their parents have discovered they'd been drinking?
12 Which one was the most successful at ballroom dancing?

Exercise 2

Make each of the following phrases and sentences negative.

1 We went into the fourth year.
2 Nigel started going to ballroom dancing.
3 His mother's mother knew Rosalie.
4 I had been in hospital.
5 We both went along.
6 We used to cycle down . . .
7 There were quite a few girls . . .
8 Graham's very good.

🎧 **Exercise 3**

Listen to Exercise 3 on your tape and write down what Nigel says.

10.2 Julia remembers her early childhood.

Ray has just told his friends that he can remember sitting in his pram with people looking at him! No-one believes that anyone can remember so far back and so everyone begins to try to recollect their very earliest memories.

Points of detail

a high-chair — a chair with especially long legs in which you seat a small child

concrete — made with cement and sand, and very hard

two or so — two years old or a little more, e.g. 'Can you wait an hour or so and then it'll be finished?

Rayburn — a make of kitchen stove

tiles — flat pieces of clay, or other material, used for covering floors, walls, roofs, etc.

Jersey — one of the Channel Islands, small islands between England and France

Kingston — a town to the west of London

Mount Ararat Road — a street in Richmond, also to the west of London

bed-sitter — a one-room flat

times were quite hard — life was difficult

broomsticks — the handle of the broom (i.e. the brush used for sweeping the floor)

Aladdin heater — a make of small paraffin heater

clippings — here, newspaper cuttings, pieces cut out of the newspaper because they are of special interest to someone

The Richmond and Twickenham Times — i.e. the local weekly newspaper

blaze — fire

beaming smile — a very big smile

Exercise 1

Answer each of the following questions by choosing the most appropriate answer from A B C or D.

1 Julia remembers
   A being in a high-chair
   B being two
   C what happened to the high-chair
   D falling out of her pram

2 She fell on to
   A a high chair   C the floor
   B the carpet   D the Rayburn

3 When she was two, Julia moved to
   A Kingston Hospital   C Mount Ararat Road
   B Richmond   D Jersey

4 Her parents lived in a bed-sitter because
   A there was a war on
   B it was near the hospital
   C they didn't have much money
   D they didn't like Richmond

5 One day, when Julia's mother was ironing
   A she had an Aladdin heater
   B she fell over the heater
   C the ironing board fell over the heater
   D the sheet fell over the heater

6 The picture in the newspaper showed
   A Julia alone   C Julia and her mother
   B Julia's parents   D Julia and her parents

Exercise 2

*Find a word or phrase on the tape for which each of the
following words or phrases in italics is an explanation.*

1 So that's what *occurred*!
2 *Honestly*?
3 that's all I *recollect*
4 *nasty*
5 because we *went to live* there
6 times were quite *difficult*
7 to *beat* on the ceiling
8 that make pretty *designs*
9 it was very *alarming*
10 'Baby saved from *fire*!'

Exercise 3

*Try to explain what each of the following newspaper
headlines might mean.*
Example: BABY SAVED FROM BLAZE.
Answer: A baby who was in a house which caught fire
        was saved by her mother.

1 CRIME WAVE IN CITY
2 PICASSO FETCHES £70,000
3 OLD PEOPLE HARD HIT BY COLD
4 STRIKE OVER WORKING CONDITIONS
5 ENTRY BY BRICK

6   HIJACK HOSTAGE KILLED IN BID TO ESCAPE
7   SMASH AND GRAB — ATTEMPT FOILED
8   ENGLAND FORWARDS TEAR DEFENCE APART

Exercise 4

*Ask a lot of people what their earliest memory is and write
their answers down, like this:*
    being put in a bath which was too hot
    seeing a new dog
*Try to get everyone to tell you at what age each thing
happened and then decide how far back people seem to be
able to remember.*

10.3 Ray and Isabel look back romantically to the first time they met.

When Ray asks his wife whether she remembers the first time
she fell in love, she very cleverly replies by telling him her
memories of the first time she met *him*! They both have a
clear picture of that first meeting.

Points of detail
supermarket — large self-service shop, selling food, household
     goods, etc.
came to stay — i.e. to stay in their house for a night or more
Dubliners — people from Dublin in Ireland; but here, a well-known
     group of folksingers, some of whom have large beards
grubby — dirty, untidy
insignificant — unimpressive, not special
I thought, 'Oh dear' — Isabel leaves the thought unfinished!
mac — abbreviation for mackintosh, i.e. raincoat

Exercise 1

*Answer each of the following questions briefly with the exact
words from the tape.*

1   What exactly does Ray ask Isabel?
2   Where did Isabel used to work on Friday evenings?
3   What did Isabel already know about Ray?
4   How did Isabel look when she arrived home from work?
5   What had Ray started to call Isabel's parents by the next day?
6   What was Isabel wearing when Ray first saw her?

7 How was her hair arranged?
8 How old was Isabel then?

Exercise 2

Use each of the following phrases in italics in a sentence of your own to show that you know what it means.

1 *falling in love*
2 *the first time* I met you
3 *on Friday evenings*
4 *a friend of my brother's*
5 *with a big beard*
6 *came in from* work
7 *all grubby and dirty*
8 *quite a* surprise
9 *a lot* smaller
10 *more insignificant*
11 *Oh dear!*
12 *I'll never forget*
13 *in the doorway*
14 her hair *tied back*
15 *quite a picture*

Exercise 3

Try to write at least six lines of teenage romantic poetry. It can be a poem to send to the one you love, or a poem about a love in the past.

Can you say . . .?

Go back now to the list at the beginning of the Unit. There are a lot of expressions there which you will find useful in remembering special things about some or all of these topics:
— your first love
— your first day at school
— your teenage life (if you're old enough)
— your happiest holiday
— the days before you went to school
— how you spent Christmas as a child

11 People agreeing and disagreeing

11.1 Matthew finds that Moira and Colin share his dislike of sports.

Young people are generally expected to enjoy sport of some kind. When asked what sport he likes, Matthew says, rather hesitantly, that he's not very interested in sport. He is pleased to find that Moira and Colin are two more people for whom sport is of little interest.

Points of detail
follow — here, look at the news about
rugby — a kind of football played with an oval-shaped ball which may be handled
purely — simply, only

bet me a pint — make a bet in which the loser buys the winner a
    pint of beer
take it on — accept the challenge
for a joke — for fun
rowing — a way of moving a boat with oars (i.e. long narrow pieces
    of wood)
closely — carefully
abhor — hate
a spectator sport — a sport to watch. People who go to football
    matches etc. are called 'spectators'.
Hear, hear! — I quite agree. An expression usually used by listeners
    who agree with what a public speaker says.
hearties — a slang word meaning 'energetic people', often used in a
    mocking, scornful way
taken to — started
Kew — an area of Richmond, a small town to the west of London
Hyde Park — a large park in central London
let him loose — free him from his lead
tedious — here, annoying
fat, business expense-account lunches — large, rich lunches which
    are paid for by business accounts not by the individual who eats
    them

Exercise 1

*Answer each of the following questions using a complete
sentence for each answer.*

1 Is Matthew keen on sport?
2 Why does he follow rugby?
3 Why has he watched the rowing recently?
4 Does he do any rowing now?
5 Would he like to watch a football match?
6 What does Moira like doing for exercise?
7 What does Moira's dog want to do to the runners in Hyde
    Park?
8 What do Moira and Colin think is the reason why people run
    round the park?

Exercise 2

Use each of the words in italics in a sentence of your own.

1 *sport* doesn't interest me
2 That's *exactly* our attitude
3 *purely* because every week . . .
4 someone will *win*

5 I've watched the recent *rowing*
6 a *spectator* sport
7 *organized* sport
8 *pleasant* exercise
9 I get very *annoyed*
10 I can hardly *blame* him

Exercise 3

Each of the groups of words below is associated with a particular activity. For each group, decide what the activity is.

1 ball, goal, goal-posts
2 album, hinges, catalogue
3 wheels, saddle, handle-bars
4 rope, axe, climbing-boots
5 spade, lawn-mower, fork
6 pattern, needles, wool
7 nails, wood, hammer
8 take-off, seat-belts, wings
9 back-stroke, water, dive
10 brush, palette, paint

Exercise 4

Think of six ways of expressing dislike and then write sentences in the pattern given in the example. Make some positive and some negative if you can.
Examples: '*I loathe* pop music.' 'Yes, *I loathe* it too.'
'*I wouldn't like to* fly.' 'No, *I wouldn't like to* either.'

11.2 Bob finds that not everyone agrees with his views on cars in towns.

Bob no longer drives a car. He believes that cars have no place in busy cities, but Sarah doesn't agree with him. Jonathon isn't too sure, but suggests that public and private transport shouldn't be mixed together.

Points of detail
disabled — physically handicapped
administrative rule — here, a law which it is possible to enforce

nippy — a colloquial word for 'energetic', 'quick in movement'

drive in — here, drive in to London

subsidize — give money to a cause needing help

mini-bus — small bus

aren't *that* bad — 'that' stressed in this way is used, usually with a
  negative verb, to mean 'so very', e.g. 'I've got toothache but I'm
  not going to the dentist because it isn't *that* painful.'

you might as well — it is just as good

some other form — another kind

blocked up — crowded

by foot — Although the majority of people say 'on foot', an
  increasing number now say 'by foot'.

Tube — Underground train

an alternative — another choice

given up — here, stopped using. 'Give up' is often used to mean
  'stop' for habits which are considered bad, e.g. 'I've given up
  smoking', 'he's given up drinking.'

on the other side — here, belonging to the opposite group

has found salvation — here, has been saved from a bad thing

sinners — people who do things which are wrong

going wrong — making mistakes

strikes — when people stop working in order to get more pay, better
  conditions, etc.

utter pleasure — absolute pleasure

getting rid of — removing

efficiently — well

🎧 Exercise 1

*Answer each of the following questions by choosing the
most appropriate answer from A B C or D.*

1 Bob thinks that
   A everyone
   B everyone except those over 21
   C everyone under 65
   D everyone who is disabled
   should be forbidden to drive in the city.

2 People over 65 should have cars
   A because it's the law
   B because they are not rich
   C because they need cars
   D because they are nippy

3 Many elderly people don't use taxis because
   A they're expensive
   B they're electric
   C there are too many of them
   D they don't know the cost

4 A mini-bus system is suggested by
   A all of them   C Jonathon
   B Sarah   D none of them

5 The argument in favour of cars is put by
   A Bob   C Jonathon
   B Sarah   D none of them

6 Bob mentions three ways of travelling used by the majority of
   people. Which of the following does he *not* include?
   A on foot   C by bus
   B by Underground   D by taxi

7 Bob is happy without a car because
   A he's on the other side
   B life is better without one
   C the others are quite wrong
   D he has been saved

8 Sarah thinks that the problem is caused by
   A too many taxis   C having no taxis
   B having too mixed a system D too many cars

Exercise 2

*For each of the words and phrases in italics find a word
which is opposite in meaning. You will find all the opposites
on the tape.*

1 those *under* sixty-five
2 those over sixty-five and *physically fit*
3 *useless* administrative rule
4 to *forbid* elderly people
5 in *large* electric cars
6 *more* nippy
7 *few* elderly people
8 *young* people
9 cars aren't that *good*
10 who is *unhappy* to do it

11 life is *unhealthier*
12 . . . and *nastier*
13 the *best* drivers
14 works . . . *inefficiently*
15 *everybody* comes off best

Exercise 3

Bob refers to 'disabled' people. Many words beginning with 'dis-' are used to show lack of something. Write down the word which is used for each of the following.

1 not willing to obey
2 not organized well
3 not approving
4 refusing to believe
5 the opposite to 'advantage'
6 not satisfied
7 not to like
8 to spoil the colour

Exercise 4

Give a short answer either agreeing or disagreeing with each of the following statements.
Example: Green cars are easily seen in the dark.
Answer: No, they aren't.

1 Mushrooms grow faster at night.
2 Money has ruined you.
3 It's easier to study in the morning.
4 Pop music should be played very loudly.
5 School days are the happiest days of your life.
6 Queen Elizabeth is the most famous woman in the world.
7 Your friends were late arriving.
8 It was cold yesterday.
9 You would help me, wouldn't you?
10 Your teacher likes music, I suppose.

11.3 Simon and Tom J. try to work out the advantages of being a bachelor.

Simon is a bachelor. Tom is married. Sarah has been

suggesting that Simon has an easy life as a bachelor, but Simon isn't convinced that he has any special advantages over a married man. Tom tends to think that there may be advantages to bachelorhood!

Points of detail

speaking as — i.e. giving the point of view of, e.g. 'Speaking as a parent, I believe that life is more complicated for young people nowadays.'

single — here, unmarried

a baby-sitter — someone to look after the baby when you want to go out

missed opportunities — things that you could have done which you failed to do at the time

theoretically — in theory, not in fact

capable of taking — able to take. The verb 'take' is often used with 'opportunity', e.g. 'I would like to take this opportunity of thanking you for your help.'

the launderette — a laundry where you can wash your own clothes in automatic coin-operated washing-machines

washing — i.e. washing of clothes

trip — here, 'passport' would be another suitable word

ᐰᐰ Exercise 1

Decide whether each of these statements is true or false, according to what you have heard on the tape.

1 Simon isn't married.
2 People think being a bachelor gives you freedom.
3 Parents have to get baby-sitters when they want to go out.
4 Tom says people never understand what bachelor freedom means.
5 Simon thinks there are probably no advantages to being alone.
6 Sarah suggests a possible disadvantage.
7 Simon doesn't wash his own clothes.
8 If he was married, Simon would definitely do his own washing.

Exercise 2

Use each of the words and phrases in italics in a sentence of your own to show that you have understood the meaning.

1 *speaking as* a bachelor
2 Does one *choose*?

3   *people think that . . .*
4   you're free *in some way*
5   you *don't have to* get a baby-sitter
6   you're *no longer* free
7   *looking back on* all the missed opportunities
8   it *depends on* who you marry
9   free *housework*
10 *a bit* false

🎧 **Exercise 3**

Listen to Exercise 3 on your tape. You will hear groups of three words. Write down each group and underline the word which comes from the tape. You will hear each group twice. There are eight groups.

Exercise 4

There must be more good and bad aspects to being single than Tom and Simon talk about! List at least eight points, good or bad, and then ask someone else whether they agree with you or not.

Example: A bachelor can get up late every morning. Do you agree with me?

Can you say . . .?

Look back now at the list of expressions at the beginning of the Unit. We often find ourselves in situations where we want to agree or disagree with other people and we must sometimes be careful to disagree without being too unpleasant. Decide how strongly you want to agree or disagree and then discuss some or all of the topics below with other people.
— sports
— music
— city transport
— television
— private education
— the best way to learn English

---

12 People talking about the things they want

They say ...

The one thing I really want to do is . .
I would really like to . . .
You said you'd like to . . .
I want to walk
I want to do some bicycle riding
I want to get some exercise
I would like to be able to . . .
Would you like that?
I don't think I would like that, really

I want to buy a house
That's what I want to do
I wish to find somewhere to live
You hope to arrange all these things?
I'm hoping I shall find a house

We wanted a little one
I fancy a . . .
I think my mother would fancy a . . .
I don't think I particularly want one
I don't think she wanted . . .
You'd like a . . ., wouldn't you?

12.1 Ray and Isabel consider what they want to do on their holiday.

Ray and Isabel and their friends are discussing how they're going to spend their holidays. Some people like an energetic holiday, others prefer something lazy and relaxing. Ray has obviously thought a lot about what he wants to do on his holiday.

Points of detail

places rather than castles — Isabel wants to see interesting
  geographical areas, rather than go to places of historical
  importance.

going over to some of the islands — Ray and Isabel are going to
  Scotland for their holiday. There are lots of small islands off the
  coast of Scotland and Isabel would like to go, by boat, to visit
  some of them.

a bit too close to home — an idiomatic expression meaning that it
  would cause an uncomfortable feeling

Exercise 1

*Answer each of the following questions, using a short but
complete sentence for each answer.*

1 Has Ray had a lot of experience of fishing?
2 Why does Ray think fishing would be good for him?
3 What exercise does Isabel want to have?
4 What would prevent Isabel from swimming?
5 Is Isabel interested in castles?
6 What does Ray consider to be good exercise?
7 Does Ray want to use the car a lot?
8 Does Isabel want to eat the fish Ray plans to catch?

Exercise 2

*Find the word or phrase on the tape for which each of the
following words or phrases in italics is an explanation.*

1 I would *particularly enjoy being* able to . . .
2 to do something *of that sort*
3 castles and *that sort of thing*
4 some of the islands, *maybe*
5 I want to do some *cycling*
6 we could get *a longer way*
7 to *hook* fish

Exercise 3

*Listen to Exercise 3 on your tape and write down exactly
what Ray says.*

Exercise 4

Imagine that you are going to the countryside (not the

*seaside) for a holiday and list five things you want to do.
Put each one in a different sentence, using expressions from
the beginning of the Unit to help you.*

12.2 Simon wants to buy a house.

Tom asks Simon what plans he has for the summer,
expecting to talk of holidays. Simon, however, has spent
such a long time abroad that he now feels a strong desire to
have a home of his own. Tom treats the whole matter in a
very lighthearted way, but Simon is obviously anxious to buy
himself a house.

Points of detail
living out of suitcases — Simon has moved around a lot and has
   therefore lived in many different places, using suitcases to carry
   his possessions.
2.4 children — the average size of family in England is 2.4 children.
   Notice the use of the word 'point' to indicate the decimal. It is
   written as a full-stop.
a couple of summers — two summers
to exchange contracts — to complete the formal arrangements for
   buying a house
a lengthy process — a long series of actions

Exercise 1

*Decide whether each of these statements is true or false,
according to what you have heard Tom and Simon say.*

1 Simon wants to rent a house.
2 Simon has slept in a suitcase for most of his life.
3 He came back to England last year.
4 Simon is unemployed.
5 Simon wants to have a house this year.
6 He will not consider buying a flat.
7 He hopes to find something to buy before September.
8 It takes quite a long time to complete the arrangements for
   buying a house in England.

Exercise 2

*Use each of the following phrases in italics in a sentence of
your own to show that you understand the meaning.*

1 *a home*
2 I've spent *most of* my life
3 *I wish* to find
4 *next,* you'll have your house
5 *Which comes first?*
6 *I don't know*
7 you hope to *arrange*
8 *allowing yourself* a couple of summers
9 *I'm hoping* I shall . . .
10 *by* September

Find the word on the tape for which each of the following words or phrases in italics is an explanation.

1 I *came back* to England
2 *a year ago*
3 a *regular, full-time* job
4 I *want* to find
5 to live *completely* on my own
6 *Next* will you have a wife?
7 you hope to *fix* all these things
8 *permitting* yourself a couple of summers
9 *two* summers
10 a *long* process

Exercise 4

Imagine you are about to get married and are not very rich. Put the items below in the order in which you would buy them, remembering that you may have to wait a number of years before you can afford the things you put at the bottom of your list!

a television set	a refrigerator
bedroom furniture	a washing-machine
a cooker	a dish-washer
a car	armchairs
garden tools	carpets
new clothes	curtains
a dining-table and chairs	a typewriter

12.3 Colin and Moira enquire about what sort of weddings Matthew and Lucy want to have.

Mary is about to go to a wedding and asks Colin and Moira their views on the size of weddings. They think that it's more interesting to know what kind of wedding young people like Matthew and his sister, Lucy, would prefer. Matthew and Lucy point out that it is often not a question of what the young couple would prefer, but rather a question of what sort of wedding their parents want them to have.

Points of detail

tiny — very small
to throw away — (with reference to money) to waste, e.g. 'He throws his money away on all sorts of rubbish.'
taste — here, what people prefer to do
I fancy — I like the idea of
splash-out — extravagant, big, luxurious. The verb 'to splash out' means 'to spend a lot of money'.
a marquee — a very large tent, put up for a special occasion
resist — stop something happening
that averse — so opposed, against (see Points of Detail 11.2 'that')
go nuts — a slang expression meaning to 'go mad'

Exercise 1

Answer each of the following questions by choosing the most appropriate answer from A B C or D.

1 Colin and Moira had
   A a very small wedddding
   B a big wedding
   C a fairly small wedding
   D an average-sized wedding

2 Colin says the size of a wedding depends on
   A the couple's wishes
   B how much money you have
   C how much money you want to spend
   D taste

3 Moira would have
   A hated
   B loved
   C wanted
   D liked
   a big wedding for herself.

4 Matthew wants
   A a very small wedding
   B a big wedding
   C a fairly small wedding
   D an average-sized wedding

5   Lucy's mother would want her to have
    A a very small wedding   C a fairly small wedding
    B a big wedding   D an average-sized wedding

6   Lucy gives her view on the size of wedding she would like.
    A She's determined to have a huge wedding whatever her
       parents think.
    B She isn't going to get married.
    C She's so anxious to have a small wedding that she
       wouldn't get married otherwise.
    D She's not keen on a big wedding, but wouldn't mind
       much.

7   Colin and Moira's daughter got married last year. She had
    A a big wedding   C a quiet wedding
    B a noisy wedding   D a fairly big wedding

8   Lucy expects her mother to say
    A 'You'd like to get married, dear, wouldn't you?'
    B 'You'd like a big wedding, dear, wouldn't you?'
    C 'Oh dear, you can't have a big wedding.'
    D 'You'd like a small, quiet wedding, dear, wouldn't you?'

Exercise 2

*Give an explanation for each of the following as it is used on
the tape.*

1   a tiny wedding
2   I'd have hated a big one
3   I don't think you can make rules about it.
4   a real splash-out wedding
5   my mother would fancy . . .
6   resist (it)
7   I'm not *that* averse
8   what individually one wants
9   a year last June
10 I'm going to have . . .

Exercise 3

Think of eight things that you want and others might not want you to do or to have. Then write sentences as in the examples.

Examples: I want to live abroad but my parents don't want me to.

I would like an aeroplane, but my mother doesn't want me to have one.

Can you say . . .?

The list at the beginning of the Unit gives a number of useful phrases for expressing wants and desires. Make use of them in talking to other people about what they or you want. Some of the topics below might be good starting points, although wants are usually very personal.

— ambitions
— shopping
— to improve the place where you live
— to enjoy your social life more
— to educate yourself

---

13 People asking for and making suggestions

13.1 Celia, Scilla and Felix suggest what to do if you can't sleep.

Celia, Scilla and Felix all have ideas about what it is best to do if you can't sleep. For one person one thing is effective, for another something else works better.

Points of detail
conventional — traditional
counting sheep — It is lightheartedly believed that if you can't sleep you should imagine sheep in a field and count them as they walk through the gate or even as they jump over the hedge!

resist — fight against

mental arithmetic — calculations which can be done in your head, without writing the numbers down

laid awake — Felix should have said 'lain awake'. Many English people confuse the verbs 'to lie' and 'to lay'.

snoring away — 'to snore' is to breath noisily while sleeping

get to the point — arrive at the situation

get to sleep — fall asleep

Exercise 1

Make a list of all the suggestions which Celia, Scilla and Felix make. Write each one in a sentence. There are about ten suggestions.

Examples: 1. Drinking whisky is a conventional suggestion for getting to sleep.

2. Counting sheep is quite effective if you can't get to sleep.

Exercise 2

Find the word or phrase on the tape for which each of the following words or phrases in italics is an explanation.

1 sleeping *tablets*
2 the *wish* to stay awake
3 you *clearly* are awake
4 so *leave your bed* and do something
5 *never mind how* early in the morning
6 however *peculiar* it may be
7 don't *be concerned* about not sleeping
8 *it's not really important* at all
9 something that is very *agreeable*
10 places that you would like to *visit*
11 mental arithmetic *questions*
12 they're so *difficult* that . . .
13 I never get them *completed*
14 (it) takes me *a very long time* to get up
15 it's very *annoying* if . . .

Exercise 3

Make a list of ten more suggestions you could make to people who find it difficult to sleep.

Exercise 4

*There are a number of time words and phrases in the
discussion. Write down six of them.*

13.2 Ray, Isabel and Julia consider what people can do with any extra money they have.

People's ideas vary about what to do with any extra money
one has. Older people generally believe that young people
should save their money, but not all young people agree. Ray
suggests investment as a good use of money, but Isabel and
Julia have different views on what one might invest the
money in.

Points of detail
over — i.e. left over, remaining after you have paid for the things
    you need. Used also for other things, e.g. 'Who'll eat these other
    potatoes? There are two left over.'
pay — wages or salary
invest — spend it on something that will increase in value
inflation is running very high — i.e. money is quickly losing its value
devalue — become worthless
sum — amount, quantity
you are left — here, 'left' means 'given' money in a will when
    somebody dies, e.g. 'He died last week and left all his money to a
    dogs' home.'
legacy — something left to somebody in a will
in its own terms — in its own way
hold on to — keep
right away — immediately
electrical goods — things which are operated by electricity

⌒⌒ **Exercise 1**

*Decide whether each of these statements is true or false,
according to what Ray, Isabel or Julia say.*

1 Ray thinks it's a good idea to invest money.
2 Money is decreasing in value.
3 Isabel doesn't agree with investing a regular amount of
   money.
4 If you have £200 left to you, Isabel says you should buy
   something with it.
5 Some people invest in wine.

6   Ray knows just how long you should keep money before spending it.
7   People seem to be spending their money immediately.
8   People are buying goods which they might not be able to afford now.

Exercise 2

Use each of the following phrases in italics in a sentence of your own to show that you know what it means.

1   *extra money over* from your pay
2   *each month*
3   you should *invest* it
4   *even though* inflation is running very high
5   *that's true*
6   it's a *regular* sum
7   you're *left* £200
8   buy *something special*
9   *in some ways*, that can be more valuable
10 *in that case* you should spend it

Exercise 3

Listen to Exercise 3 on your tape and write down what Isabel says.

Exercise 4

Think of ten things that you own and pretend that you are making your will. Write down who should inherit each of the things.
Example: I leave my books to my niece, Janet, who
            reads a lot.

13.3 Bob would like to know how people get a ladder when they want one.

When Bob wants to get up on to the roof to do repairs, he is always in difficulty because he hasn't got a ladder. He has thought of some possibilities for getting a ladder for himself. Jonathon and Sarah provide some more, not very helpful, suggestions.

Points of detail

roofs — Although the plural of 'roof' is 'roofs', Bob, like many English people, says 'rooves', making the same kind of plural as 'hoof, hooves'.

first and second floors — In Britain the bottom floor of a house is called 'the ground floor'; the floors above are the first, second, third, etc.

unfortunately — Bob is speaking rather quickly and so you don't hear the 'un' before 'fortunately'.

own one — have one

to hire — to rent, to borrow for a payment

hire-shop — There are shops which specialize in hiring out all the things that a person may need to do jobs on his house, etc.

blocked gutters — The pipes which carry water around the roof are full of rubbish which stops the water flowing.

the odd mislocated tile — 'the odd' means, in this case, 'one or two'. Another example: 'Have you got the odd pound to lend me, please?'

mislocated — not in it's right place

tile — flat brick used on a roof

coping — Coping is the line of V-shaped tiles which is put over the top edge of the roof to stop water going through.

insoluble — impossible to find a solution

move — i.e. move to another house

a co-operative — a group which joins together for some special purpose

to go in with you — here, a colloquial expression meaning 'to share in buying'

Exercise 1

Answer each of the following questions as briefly as possible (with just a word, or a few words).

1 Why does Bob want a long ladder?
2 Does Bob have a ladder?
3 Why doesn't Bob buy a ladder?
4 How many of Bob's friends have a long ladder?
5 What is Bob's problem if he decides to hire a ladder?
6 Why doesn't he put it on his car?
7 How far is it from the hire-shop to Bob's flat?
8 What's the matter with the gutters on Bob's roof?
9 And some of the tiles?
10 What is the only solution Bob can find?
11 How many people can Bob find who want a ladder at the same time as he does?
12 What is the only thing left to do?

⌾ **Exercise 2**

Find the word or phrase on the tape for which each of the following words or phrases in italics is an explanation.

1 the *principal difficulty* is . . .
2 *on two occasions during the year*
3 *a great deal of* money
4 it's *not possible* to get the ladder
5 you can't *repair* your roof
6 it's *impossible to find an answer*
7 *a very small number of* people really want to . . .
8 *six months later*

Exercise 3

Bob says that some tiles on his roof are 'mislocated'. Write down a word beginning with 'mis-' for which each of the following is an explanation.

1 behave badly
2 send somebody the wrong way
3 put something in the wrong place
4 not understand correctly
5 judge somebody incorrectly
6 count wrongly
7 print incorrectly
8 pronounce wrongly

Can you say . . .?

Go back now to the list at the beginning of the Unit. You will have noticed that people make suggestions in many different ways, sometimes saying what they do or think themselves, sometimes putting forward ideas that they have heard of. Practise making suggestions on some, or all, of these topics:
— how to spend time on a journey
— disciplining the young
— what your government could do
— preventing inflation
— stopping people smoking

---

14 People talking about what they prefer

They say . . .

I prefer them to the last ones
Yeah, they're better, those
Don't you think they suit her more?

I would prefer a sincere affair
I would prefer to see the money spent on . . .
If they prefer a large wedding . . .
If they prefer to invite . . .
I would prefer . . . rather than . . .
I think it's more genuine and more intimate

What would you prefer?
Yes, now that would interest me
Would that be your favourite holiday?
That would be my option
What would it be, then?
I'd rather go on a yacht than on . . .
It would be much more exciting
I would much rather do some sailing rather than . . .

14.1 Susan and Sarah want to know if Mary's new glasses are an improvement.

Mary has got some new glasses which are a completely different shape from any she has had before. Her daughters are very conscious of how different she looks, so when Tom and Simon come to visit them, they ask them what they think of the new glasses. Everyone seems to think that they are better than the ones she used to wear.

Points of detail
pairs of owls — slang use of 'owls' to mean glasses. Sarah probably uses the word 'owls' because the lenses of the new glasses are very circular, like an owl's eyes!

different to before — Sarah should say 'different *from* before', but many people say 'different to'.
they suit you — they look good on you
photochromic — Susan gives an explanation of this word on the tape.
in theory — Susan says 'in theory' because the sun has not shone since Mary got the glasses, so they don't know yet whether it's true in practice!
What's the point? — i.e. What's the purpose?
dazzled — unable to see clearly because there is too much light
darken up — get darker

Exercise 1

Answer each of the following questions by choosing the most appropriate answer from A B C or D according to what you have heard on the tape.

1 Tom thinks Mary
  A looks very different in her new glasses
  B isn't wearing new glasses
  C doesn't look different in her new glasses
  D shouldn't wear new glasses

2 Mary's new glasses are
  A smaller
  B more square
  C more circular
  D thinner
  than her old ones.

3 Photochromic means that in the sun the glasses
  A get thicker
  B get lighter
  C get paler
  D get darker

4 Photochromic also means that in the dark they
  A get thicker
  B get darker
  C get thinner
  D get paler

5 The photochromic properties of the glasses haven't been tested yet because
  A Mary hasn't worn them
  B the sun hasn't shone since she bought them
  C the rain spoils them
  D Mary doesn't have to wear glasses in the dark

6   The reason for having photochromic lenses is
     A to have more pairs of glasses
     B to wear sun-glasses all the time
     C not to have to wear glasses when standing in the dark
     D not to have to change glasses when going into the sun

Exercise 2

Write down a word opposite in meaning to each of the following words in italics from the tape.

1   Does she look *different*?
2   they're very *nice*
3   I *like* them
4   they suit you extremely *well*
5   I think they're *good*
6   a bit *bigger*
7   they were *longer*
8   they're *better*
9   they go *dark*
10   when they *darken*

Exercise 3

Make a list of ten things you could do to alter your appearance.
Example: grow a beard

Exercise 4

Draw a rough sketch of the shape of glasses which you think would suit you and then write a brief description of the shape you have drawn.

14.2 Julia and Ray say what kind of weddings they prefer.

Julia prefers a wedding that is sincere and meaningful and not just an opportunity for parents to show off. Ray doesn't think her attitude is fair to parents and believes that they have the right to choose what kind of wedding their daughter should have. Isabel, who has listened quietly so far, adds her view at the end.

114

Points of detail

affair — event
meaningful — significant, having some meaning
showy — all done to show how rich you are
prestigious — for prestige, i.e., here, to show how important the
    parents are
show off — to make a display of wealth, beauty, etc.
Auntie Flo and Uncle Bill — here used to suggest relatives who the
    young person would not wish to invite because they are distant
    relatives
prerogative — special privilege
it boils down to — a colloquial expression, meaning 'it is simply a
    matter of'
consulted — asked what they think
in perspective — in proper relation to each other
genuine — real, lacking in pretence
categories — types, kinds
intimate — close, personal
display of wedding presents — At some weddings, all the gifts
    which the couple has received are put on show for everyone to
    see.

Exercise 1

*Decide whether each of these statements is true or false,
according to the conversation.*

1   Julia prefers large weddings.
2   She likes showy weddings.
3   Parents, in Ray's view, have a right to show off.
4   The parents generally pay for weddings.
5   Julia would think that having a big wedding was a good way
    to spend money.
6   Parents' preferences are important to Ray.
7   Parents' preferences are the most important thing to Julia.
8   A wedding day is important for parents as well as for the
    couple who are getting married.
9   Isabel prefers small weddings.
10 She likes people to be forced to come.

Exercise 2

*Find the word or phrase on the tape for which each of the
following words or phrases in italics is an explanation.*

1   *a small number of* people
2   to *exhibit* what they can provide
3   *give to* their daughter

4　*permitted* to do this
5　the parents are *financing* it
6　*a lot* to say about it
7　not *completely*
8　they (should) be *asked what they think*
9　as *significant* a day for parents as . . .
10　*comment on* what you're wearing

🎧 **Exercise 3**

Listen to Exercise 3 on your tape. You will hear ten phrases from the conversation. Write each one down. You will hear each one twice.

14.3　Tom J. and Simon prefer other things to world cruises.

Sarah is trying to discover what Tom and Simon consider to be an ideal holiday. She imagines that a world cruise would be perfect, but, to her surprise, finds that neither Tom nor Simon agree with her. They express preferences for other types of holiday.

Points of detail
regard — look upon, consider
uniquely — Tom says uniquely (meaning, here, particularly)
　　because he intended to say 'uniquely boring'.
boring — uninteresting
stuck — kept, unable to leave
the Channel — the sea between the coasts of England and France
survive — live through
Bukhara — a town in the south west of the USSR
Inner Mongolia — a region of northern China
option — choice
just a metaphor — here, simply an example, a way of saying
　　something
yacht — a sailing boat
big ocean liner — a large ship which crosses seas

🎧 **Exercise 1**

Answer each of the following questions, using a complete sentence for each answer.

1　Would Tom or Simon like to go on a world cruise?
2　Who is enthusiastic about a trip by camel?

3 Would Tom go alone on a camel ride?
4 What would Simon do to pass the time on a world cruise?
5 What sort of story would Simon like to write?
6 How would Simon expect to feel after three days of a world cruise?
7 Why doesn't Simon like riding on camels?
8 How would Simon prefer to travel?

Exercise 2

Below are some extracts from the tape. Use each one as the beginning of a short sentence of your own.

1 I would regard . . .
2 Even if someone was paying me . . .
3 Basically . . .
4 I get bored . . .
5 I'd go with . . .
6 I think it . . .
7 Actually, . . .
8 Well, if I . . .
9 The only reason for . . .
10 I don't enjoy . . .
11 I'd rather . . .
12 I agree with . . .

Exercise 3

Choose one word from each of the two lists below, and put them together in a sentence like the one shown in the example.
Example: I prefer *jazz* to *pop music*.

tea	pop music
apples	dogs
jazz	blondes
gold	day
cats	postcards
brunettes	autumn
trains	silver
letters	oranges
spring	coffee
night	cars

Exercise 4

Write eight sentences in the pattern given in the example to express your preferences about ways of travelling.
Example: I would rather travel by plane than by boat, because flying is faster.

Can you say . . .?

Looking back at the list of expressions at the beginning of the Unit will help you express your preferences about some of the topics listed below. Remember that *how* you say things helps to show your preference, as you will have noticed particularly in listening to Tom and Simon.
— living in the town or in the country
— large cars or small cars
— how many children to have
— holidays abroad or in your own country
— an indoor or an outdoor job

---

15 People complaining and criticizing

They say . . .

It's deteriorated
She has no idea that . . .
Some days you only have . . .
It's very strange
I don't like the idea of salad
So many times I want to have . . .
They're a bit . . .
You can't choose . . .
That's revolting
It's horrible
It's the planning that's so bad
Now, they don't seem to . . .
The choice is really bad sometimes
You wonder why they bother
Why they don't give it to us . . .
What seems so silly is that . . .

It's not even O.K. for me
It's stupid
It's ridiculous
very, very expensive

I think the Underground's got much worse
There are fewer trains . . .
more of a squash
And it's very expensive
It seems so ridiculous to . . .
Buses are far worse
Why is it that, on buses, there is always somebody . . .?
There's nothing more annoying
I think it's awful

15.1 Lucy, Sarah and Avril, complain about school dinners.

Schools in England provide lunch for all children who want it because the normal school day is from about nine o'clock in the morning until four in the afternoon. Although the meal is, in fact, 'lunch', it is nearly always referred to as 'school dinner'. The meals are planned to give a properly balanced diet and there is usually a choice of dishes, but almost all school-children complain about them whether they are good or bad. Lucy feels that school dinners have got worse in the last year and soon Sarah and Avril join in with all the criticisms they have.

Points of detail
deteriorated — got worse
has no idea — doesn't understand
a roll — i.e. a bread roll
hot plate — a heated surface from which hot dishes are served. In their school, salads and hot dishes are now served from different places and so it isn't possible to have salad with a hot dish, as it used to be before.
ravioli — an Italian dish of pasta, meat and sauce
ready-made — prepared in advance
beetroot — a dark red salad vegetable
non-existent — here, not substantial, small
white-washed rice — here, Avril means rice that has been boiled for too long and is tasteless.
soggy — wet
gritty — with bits of stone in it
caterpillar — the larva of a butterfly
revolting — disgusting, horrible
in charge — responsible
erratic — unreliable
a knack — a special skill
loads — colloquial for 'lots'

Exercise 1

Answer each of the following questions by choosing the most appropriate answer from A B C or D, according to what you have heard the girls say.

1   The meals this year are
A a bit better
B a lot worse
C a lot better
D a little worse
than they were before.

2   The new lady in charge of school dinners
    A   doesn't like school-girls
    B   hasn't been a cook before
    C   works in industry
    D   worked in industry before

3   Sarah has noticed that nice things are
    A   always served on the same day
    B   never served at all
    C   always kept to eat with salad
    D   always served by the lady herself

4   None of the girls likes not being able to
    A   eat salad alone   C   eat salad and a hot dish
    B   eat early   D   eat two hot dishes

5   Avril doesn't eat lettuce at school, because once she
    A   found a fly in her lettuce
    B   found a caterpillar in her lettuce
    C   found grit in her lettuce
    D   found beetroot in her lettuce

6   The cause of the trouble is
    A   the amount the girls eat   C   lack of planning
    B   preparing too much   D   lack of money

7   There is often a shortage of choice when the last girls come
    to lunch because
    A   there is not enough food prepared
    B   before they used to do too much
    C   the food is being kept for the next day
    D   they only keep things that are easy to keep

8   Avril thinks it is silly that the staff prepare lots of the kinds of
    food that
    A   are spongy   C   everybody likes
    B   nobody likes   D   they like themselves

Exercise 2

Write a brief explanation for each of the following words and phrases from the tape.

1   has come from industry
2   you're no less hungry
3   yes, exactly

4   when they can't afford
5   it's very strange
6   so many times
7   their ready-made salads
8   the people who do the lunch
9   they make an effort
10 it's so erratic

Exercise 3

Find a word which rhymes with each of the words below and then give an explanation of the word you find. If you are not sure about the sound of a word on the list, you can find it on the tape.
Example: thing
Answer: wing — part of a bird

1	whole	8	places
2	half	9	times
3	days	10	leaf
4	five	11	money
5	feed	12	keep
6	strange	13	bad
7	nice	14	knack

Exercise 4

There must be things that you find/found irritating at school. Include eight of these things in sentences, complaining about each one. The list of phrases at the beginning of the Unit will be useful.
Example: Why was it that, every night, we had to
           do homework?

15.2   Alec and Maureen grumble about library fines.

All towns in England have a public library from which books may be borrowed for reading at home. How much people are charged for the late return of library books varies from library to library, but Maureen finds her library expensive and feels it's particularly unfair to old people. Alec, as a trained librarian, knows more about the system of library fines than Maureen and Chris do.

Points of detail

when they've got a book out — i.e. out of the library

pension — the regular payment of money to old people by the state

discretionary — i.e. the librarians can choose whether to charge fines or not

the counter — in a library, the place from which books are issued

during my course — when I was a student

Ealing — here, Ealing public library

5p — i.e. five pence. Many people use the expression 'p' as a short form of 'pence'

due back — expected back. A date usually two or three weeks ahead is stamped (i.e. printed) in library books when you borrow them from the library. This is the date by which the book must be returned to the library.

pouring with rain — raining very heavily

you were fined — i.e. you had to pay a fine

halfpenny — half a penny

depriving anyone — preventing anyone else from having

Exercise 1

Decide whether each of these statements is true or false, according to what you have heard.

1 Maureen finds library fines expensive.
2 Old people sometimes forget to return their library books.
3 Old people must always pay fines.
4 All library assistants always charge fines.
5 Alec never borrows books from the public library.
6 He stopped when it rained.
7 He thinks the library fines at Ealing are high.
8 Fines are charged at Ealing library for any part of a week.
9 Alec remembers paying much less at his old local library.
10 The old library used to send someone to fetch the books from Alec.

Exercise 2

Find the word or phrase on the tape for which each of the following words or phrases in italics is an explanation.

1 they don't get out *so frequently*
2 they *don't remember*
3 *such a lot* of money
4 *the majority of* old people
5 they just won't *trouble* to ask for it
6 I never *take books out of* a public library

7   Ealing *increased the fines*
8   the day they were *expected* back
9   the *next* day
10   it's *stupid*

 Exercise 3

Listen to Exercise 3 on your tape. You will hear groups of three words. Write down each group, underlining the word you have heard in the conversation. You will hear each group twice. There are twelve groups.

Exercise 4

Write a short paragraph of complaint about a library or a shop, mentioning such things as what it offers, the quality of the service, the hours of opening, etc.

15.3   Simon and Tom J. complain about public transport in London.

Simon is very fed up with the Underground both from the point of view of service and because it is so expensive. Tom agrees, but adds that buses are even worse than the Underground. Simon finds a lot wrong with bus travel too.

Points of detail
the Underground — i.e. the underground railway service in London
a squash — crowded
Waterloo — a station south of the River Thames
Trafalgar Square — a station in central London
get around — here, move around
10p — 'p' is used for 'pence'
a few hundred yards — a yard is a little less than a metre.
charging — making people pay
fare — a price for travelling, e.g. 'I'll have to walk. I can't afford the bus fare.'
standard — here, fixed, not varying
Paris — Paris also has an underground railway system, known as the Métro.
set — Tom was going to say 'set price', meaning a fixed amount
outer London — the areas on the outside edges of London

Exercise 1

Answer each of the following questions using a complete sentence for each answer.

1 What two advantages does Simon mention about the Underground system nowadays?
2 What happened to Tom on his way from Waterloo to Trafalgar Square?
3 Is it far from Waterloo to Trafalgar Square?
4 What would be impossible if the Underground didn't exist?
5 Why does Simon sometimes walk instead of taking the Underground?
6 Which city does Tom mention as having a fixed price on its Underground trains?
7 Who would prefer the French system?
8 What does Tom think of buses compared with the Underground?

Exercise 2

Give another word or phrase for each of the words and phrases in italics below. They are all taken from the conversation.

1 the Underground's *got much worse*
2 there are *fewer* trains
3 *there's more of a squash*
4 it's very *expensive*
5 you *simply* couldn't get around
6 I sometimes *walk*
7 if they're very *close*
8 it seems so *ridiculous*
9 the idea of *charging so much*
10 who wants to *complain* about the fare

Exercise 3

Listen to Exercise 3 on your tape and write down exactly what Simon says.

Exercise 4

Make a brief list of all the things you might criticize about public transport where you live.

126

Can you say . . .?

You will have noticed that *how* you say something, as well as your actual words, will show your listener that you are complaining. The expressions at the beginning of the Unit will help you, but almost anything can be turned into a complaint; so, taking care with *how* you say things, complain — more or less angrily — about some or all of these topics:
- your parents attitude to you/your children's attitude to you
- the length of your working day
- modern books
- the quality of goods in the shops
- the behaviour of other road users

16 People talking about what must be done

They say . . .

You are required to . . .
You must stop
You must report it to the police
The safest thing is to . . .
You don't have to . . .
You must leave everything . . ., musn't you?
The most sensible thing is to . . .

You're not obliged to keep up friendships
You're obliged to keep up family ties
It should be the other way round
purely as a sense of duty
They feel obliged to . . .

We ought to shut all the windows
We ought really to . . .
Do you think we ought to . . .?
I think we should do that
We ought to do that
We ought also to make sure that . . .

16.1 Tim O., Graham and Nigel go over what people must do when a road accident happens.

Graham believes that you must always report a road accident to the police. Tim and Nigel don't agree with him, and tell him that there are only certain conditions under which reporting to the police is necessary.

Points of detail
not so — not true, not the case
settle it — come to an arrangement
privately — here, between you, without asking the police for help

any injury — if somebody is hurt
safest — here, the most sensible
bloke — slang for 'man'
wants to take action — i.e. wants to accuse you of dangerous
    driving or something like that
prosecuted — have a legal case brought against you
it's up to you — you can decide for yourself, e.g. '*I* wouldn't buy
    that car, but it's up to you — it's your money.'
causing congestion — preventing the traffic from moving
witnesses — people who saw what happened
evaluate — decide what they think of it

⌒ Exercise 1

*Answer each of the following questions using a complete
sentence for each answer.*

1 When is it essential to report an accident to the police?
2 What must you do first if you are involved in an accident?
3 Does a policeman always have to come to see an accident?
4 Why would you leave everything alone and not move
  anything until the police arrived?
5 Why did Tim move his motor-bike after he was in an
  accident?
6 Are witnesses important?

⌒ Exercise 2

*Tim and Graham use a lot of words which are particularly
appropriate to road accidents and the police. Write down at
least eight of these words from the tape.*

Exercise 3

*Write a notice which lists all the things that should be done
in case of fire. Begin:*
In Case of Fire:
1 Close all windows
2 . . . .

Exercise 4

Use all the words below in one sentence.

driver — accident — hurt — required — stop — report —
police

16.2 Bob and Jonathon consider why they visit their relatives.

Sarah asks Bob why he goes to visit his relatives and a discussion begins about whether people visit their relatives out of a sense of obligation or just because they want to do so.

Points of detail

for instance — for example
curious — peculiar, strange
the odd thing — the strange thing
blood relations — members of a family
friendships — good relations between friends
family ties — connections between members of a family
the public rule — here, the thing that people generally agree should
   be done
voluntary — done willingly, not because of obligation
offer yourself — say you are willing to do something
contract — an agreement to do something
different fields — here, different positions
attracted to them — want to see them
got out of — achieved by, gained from
as a sense of duty — feeling that you must do it
specific — special, particular

Exercise 1

Decide whether each of these statements is true or false, according to what Bob and Jonathon say.

1 Bob likes visiting his relatives.
2 Bob sees his sister nearly every week.
3 She lives twenty miles from her husband.
4 Bob finds it hard to understand why people feel the need to visit their relatives.
5 Sarah feels that one is obliged to keep up friendships.
6 You can't choose your parents.
7 People often visit their relatives at Christmas.
8 Bob has some older relatives who feel obliged to visit him.

Exercise 2

Find the word or phrase on the tape for which each of the following words or phrases in italics is an explanation.

1 *in part* obligation, in part pleasure

2 partly *enjoyment*
3 *not in keeping* with any normal visit
4 the *peculiar* thing
5 why it *occurs* at all
6 there's no *apparent* reason for it
7 there's no *special* reason for it
8 to keep up *family connections*
9 it should be *the reverse*
10 your *mother and father* are what you're given
11 you do it purely *because you feel you have to*
12 you do it *annually*

Exercise 3

Think of all the family commitments you have and write a sentence about each one, following the pattern in the example below.
Example: I must get a birthday card and send it to
            my brother for July 12th.

Exercise 4

Make a list of all relatives you have. Try to find the nearest equivalent English name to those of your relatives!
Examples: My sisters — Mary and Susan
            My uncles — Tom, . . .

16.3   Ray and Isabel list the things they must do before going on holiday.

Ray and Isabel are going to go on holiday in a few days. They realize that there are a number of little jobs to do before they go and so start making a list so that nothing will be forgotten. Julia reminds them of one or two things they should put on their list.

Points of detail
securely — safely
draw the curtains — close the curtains
slightly — a little bit
from one end — i.e. of the house

milk and papers are cancelled — Both newspapers and milk are
  delivered daily to houses in Britain, and so Isabel and Ray must
  tell the milkman and the paper-boy not to deliver any while they
  are away.
turning off — switching off
next-of-kin — nearest relatives
burglars — people who enter houses at night to steal things
implements — tools
breaking in — getting in by breaking windows or doors
stow them away — put them away safely
First Aid Kit — a box containing things that are useful if someone
  has an accident

Exercise 1

*List everything Ray and Isabel have to do before they set off
for their holiday. You should find at least twelve things.*

Exercise 2

*Now write the list of things you would have to do before
going on holiday.*

Exercise 3

*Ray and Isabel will have to tell the milkman that they don't
want any milk. Complete the following sentences with
appropriate words.*

1 I must see the . . . . about the meat.
2 We need to tell the baker that we don't want any
   . . . . tomorrow.
3 I must let the . . . . know that I want a shampoo and set
   tomorrow.
4 Can you inform the . . . . that I won't be in class
   tomorrow, please?
5 I really must see the . . . . about my pills.
6 Somebody must ask the greengrocer for some . . . .
7 I'll have to call at the . . . . for some stamps.
8 We'll have to go into the . . . . for a beer.
9 He'll have to go get his clothes washed at the . . . .
10 You have to get a ticket for the train from the . . . .

Exercise 4

A First Aid Kit contains all the little things you need if someone is injured in an accident. Underline each item from the list below which you would be likely to find in a First Aid Kit.

bandage, hammer, aspirin, fork, windscreen wiper, scissors, drill, bulb, milk, anti-septic cream, sticking plaster, flour, pencil, safety pins, ruler, saucer, folder, thermometer.

Can you say . . .?

Go back now to the list of expressions at the beginning of the Unit. Consider some, or all, of the topics below and tell your friends what you must do about them, or what *they* must do about them if you prefer!
— to clean your house
— to arrange your holiday
— to service your car
— to tidy your garden
— to buy a house
— to celebrate a special event

---

17 People asking for and giving opinions

They say . . .

It's the most savage way . . ., I think
Do you think it's all right if you . . .?
That's fine
Provided it's not somebody's cat
How far do you go?
Do you say . . .?
I don't think fishing should be allowed
I think it's criminal that . . .
I don't believe that . . .
How would you feel if . . .?

Do you think it's a good idea for children to have
  television?
In moderation, I don't see why not
I think some people . . .
There are some very good programmes on for children
I think if they just watch . . .
I think it's a bad idea to . . .
On the other hand, I think . . .
What happens . . .?
I find that . . .
That's one thing I think that . . .
perhaps

Well, I think it's remarkably clean
I tell you one thing . . .
I mean, there really aren't . . .
Yes, I agree
We should be . . .
That's something that ought to stop
Do you think the government ought to . . .?
I think the one thing that I'm very aware of . . .
I really do think it's ridiculous

17.1 Matthew gives his opinion of hunting and fishing.

Matthew replies to the question: 'Would you go hunting?' with a very strong 'No'. Moira and Colin suggest that there are some ways of hunting, and of fishing, which are perhaps less cruel than others. Matthew, however, is convinced that any kind of catching and killing of animals or fish, except for personal survival, is wrong.

Points of detail
savage — cruel
destroying — here, killing
a beast — an animal
seal-culling — killing baby seals in large numbers, so that the total population of seals does not get too big. A seal is a small, black, fish-eating sea-animal.
whale-hunting — killing whales. A whale is a large sea-animal, which is hunted for its oil and flesh.
in the spirit — here, with the intention
vermin — a wild animal which destroys things growing in the fields
cleanly shoot — here, simply shoot it, not chase after it or do anything else that is cruel
provided — on condition that
budgie — i.e. budgerigar, a small bird which some people keep in a cage in the house
rod and line — the thin straight stick and string used for fishing
in the scale — to the extent, in the quantity. Matthew says 'in the scale', though the usual expression is 'on the scale'.
criminal — here, very wicked, very wrong
hoiking — slang for 'pulling'
chucking — slang for 'throwing'
throw them back — i.e. back into the water
hook — piece of bent metal
relieved — rather less worried

⠿ Exercise 1

Answer each of the following questions using a short sentence for each answer.

1 Does Matthew approve of hunting?
2 What reason does he give for his view?
3 Would Matthew ever agree to the shooting of a rabbit?
4 Mention one thing that you really mustn't shoot!
5 Is fishing allowed in England?
6 What does Matthew think of that?
7 What does Colin believe most fishermen do with the fish they catch?

8   How does Moira think a fish feels when it's thrown back into the water?

Exercise 2

Use each of the following words and phrases in italics in a sentence of your own to show that you know what it means.

1   the most *savage* way of destroying a beast
2   *whale-hunting*
3   if you're going to eat *something like* a rabbit
4   if you go out and cleanly *shoot* it
5   *provided* it's not somebody's cat
6   your *next door neighbour*'s budgie
7   it must be *equally* painful
8   *measure*
9   *weigh*
10   *How would you feel if . . .?*

Exercise 3

Matthew obviously finds hunting and fishing cruel. Think of five things that you think are cruel and include each one in a sentence following the pattern of the example.
Example: I think it's quite wrong to keep rabbits
           in cages.

Exercise 4

How many kinds of wild animal can you think of? Make a list of at least eight.

17.2   Sarah, Lucy and Avril exchange views on whether children should watch television.

When Lucy was younger, her parents would not have television in the house. Now, the girls consider the 'pros and cons' (the advantages and disadvantages) of television for children. They all believe that there are good aspects and bad.

Points of detail
in moderation — not too much

look through — Sarah means that people look through the printed
   programmes (in the *Radio Times* and the *TV Times*, weekly
   magazines which give details about television programmes).
such and such a time — a particular time
resources — here, things you are able to do
breaks down — stops working
conversing — talking

⌒⌒ Exercise 1

*Decide whether each of these statements is true or false,
according to the views expressed by the three girls.*

1 Lucy thinks children should watch television a lot.
2 Avril says that the best programmes for children are in the
   afternoon.
3 Avril believes children shouldn't have their meals in front of
   the television.
4 Lucy thinks that setting aside special times when children
   may watch television is a good idea.
5 Avril thinks that watching television all day leaves little time
   for other activities.
6 Lucy says that on the day the television won't work you
   could do other things.
7 Sarah thinks that children don't get involved in enough
   family conversations.
8 Sarah also believes that, because of television, some children
   don't get to know their parents as much as they should.

⌒⌒ Exercise 2

*Find the word or phrase on the tape for which each of the
following words and phrases in italics is an explanation.*

1   before the week *begins*
2   if they *simply* watch . . .
3   *two* of those
4   *eat their food* in front of the television
5   until *a certain* time
6   you must *turn it off*
7   to watch it *continuously*
8   it completely *ruins*
9   the day the television *stops working*
10 or just *talking*

138

Exercise 3

Avril says that 'there are so many other things you could be doing' instead of watching television. Add at least fifteen other things to the list started by Avril.

1 reading
2 knitting
3 sewing
4 . . . .

Exercise 4

Listen to Exercise 4 on your tape and write down exactly what Lucy says.

17.3 Simon and Tom J. give Sarah their opinions on keeping Britain tidy.

Sarah feels that England has become a rather dirty country, with lots of rubbish in the streets. Although Tom and Simon think it's not as bad as some other countries, they do have some ideas on how things might be improved.

Points of detail
remarkably — surprisingly, noticeably
litter bins — rubbish containers
adjusting to — here, doing things that are made necessary by
consumer society — here, the way of life where people use
    (consume) a large number of things
overplanned — here, planned for more than were necessary
at some stage — at some time
ten yards — a yard is just less than a metre
fag-end — slang for 'cigarette-end'
packaging — wrapping things up in paper, cardboard, etc.
recycling of glassware — i.e. collecting all the used bottles, etc. and
    making them into new bottles
I'm very aware of — I notice, I see
cans — metal containers
Coca-Cola — a world-famous soft drink

Litter

DUMPING
NOT ALLOWED

🎧 Exercise 1

Answer each of the following questions by choosing the most appropriate answer from A B C or D.

1 Simon thinks England is
   A a bit dirtier than most other countries
   B a lot dirtier than most other countries
   C cleaner than most other countries
   D cleaner than when he went abroad

2 Simon finds the atmosphere in London
   A dirty
   B dirtier than when he went away
   C clean
   D cleaner than people expect

3 Tom would like to find litter bins
   A only in obvious places   C in ordinary streets
   B in every street   D in more streets

4 Tom lightheartedly suggests that Moscow had a lot of litter bins when he was there because
   A he was visiting
   B somebody ordered too many
   C too many people smoked
   D there was a stage every ten yards

5 Simon says that everything we buy
   A is cleaned up   C is litter
   B is wrapped up   D must go somewhere

6 When Simon suggests that cans are cheaper for companies to use, Tom is worried about
   A who it's cheaper for
   B who wants it to be cheaper
   C how cheap it is
   D why it needs to be cheaper

Exercise 2

Tom believes that there should be more litter bins. Consider your town and list ten places where you think there should be litter bins where there are none at present.

1 outside the ice-cream shop
2 . . . . . .

Exercise 3

In Moscow, according to Tom's remark, somebody seems to have overplanned for litter bins. Find the word beginning with 'over' for which each of the following is an explanation.

1   act in an exaggerated way
2   sleep later than you planned
3   pass somebody in a car
4   work too hard
5   hear something you were not intended to hear
6   lose your balance and fall over
7   more than normal hours of work
8   an excessive dose
9   wear clothes which are too special for the occasion
10 beat in a contest/fight

Exercise 4

Write a short paragraph describing the dirtiest place you have ever seen and giving reasons why you think it was so dirty.

Can you say . . .?

As well as using expressions which you will find by going back to the list at the beginning of this Unit, you can express opinions by the use of appropriate adjectives ('I think it's ridiculous/admirable/foolish/impossible/etc.') Talk to your friends and exchange views on some, or all, of these topics:
   — television for children/adults
   — hunting
   — how clean your town is
   — why people choose certain clothes
   — getting up early
   — loneliness
   — taking medicine

---

18 People talking about their anxieties and worries

18.1 Frank is worried about Liz swimming too far out in the sea.

Frank's own dislike and fear of the sea makes him worry a lot when he sees his wife disappearing into the distance while he stands helplessly on the beach. By the time she comes back to the beach, he is so agitated and upset that they have an argument.

Points of detail
a long way out — far away from the beach
six feet — approximately two metres
two hundred yards — approximately 180 metres
out of sight — where she can no longer be seen
gallivanting — a colloquial word meaning rushing here and there just for pleasure. 'Gallivanting' is a verb which is not used in the simple tenses.
for Christ's sake — here used as an expression of worry
miss her — here, notice that she had disappeared
hands going up — Frank is thinking of the way in which people who are drowning wave their hands in the air hoping to attract somebody's attention.
the lapping of the waves — here, the movement of the waves
rats' tails — Liz's hair is wet and 'rats' tails' describes long, wet hair which is stuck together. A rat is a small, unpleasant animal, like a mouse, but larger.
such a mess — here, so untidy
ever so — very
raging — very angry
a row — an argument, a quarrel

Exercise 1

Decide whether each of these statements is true or false, according to Frank's statements.

1 Liz swims near the beach because Frank worries about her.
2 Frank can just see Liz when she's swimming.
3 Frank follows Liz into the sea.
4 He's alone on the beach.
5 Drowning people often wave their hands in the air.
6 Liz swims without a swimming cap.
7 Frank relaxes while Liz swims.
8 Frank and Liz never argue.

Exercise 2

Find the word or phrase on the tape for which each of the following words and phrases in italics is an explanation.

1 when we go *to other countries*
2 she goes *in fact* two hundred yards
3 *where I can't see her*

4   *nearly*
5   on the *sand*
6   *in the middle of all* these other people
7   if anything *occurred*
8   this little bit of head *from time to time*
9   *more and more* worried
10 worried and *cross*
11 we have a *quarrel*

🎧 **Exercise 3**

Listen to Exercise 3 on your tape and write down what Frank says.

Exercise 4

List at least ten words associated with beaches and swimming in the sea.

18.2   Doris, in particular, is worried about police identification parades.

Many people worry about whether the police sometimes make mistakes in their attempts to catch criminals. Mary and John and their daughters are discussing recent cases with their friends, Doris and Laurie, and the question of whether people can pick out the right individual from an identification parade is a matter of concern to them all.

Points of detail
spot — pick out, select
identity parades — also called identification parades. The police find
    a number of people, place the suspected person among them and
    ask the witness to select the one he/she saw on the occasion of
    the crime.
fellow — colloquial word for 'man'
evidence — information from which to say whether someone is
    guilty or not
identification — recognizing someone by what he looks like
discounting — not depending on
go on — here, depend on
pick up — here, find out
forensic evidence — evidence used in courts of law
fingerprints — the marks made by fingers pressed on to a surface
guilty — a person who commits a crime is 'the guilty person'

145

Don't let them get away with it.
HELP THE POLICE.
If you see anything suspicious, dial 999.
Watch out!
There's a thief
ab ut

proved wrong — in the end, they were shown to be wrong
for to prove — Doris, uses 'for to prove' where most people would say simply 'to prove'.
innocent — not guilty
I gather — I understand
shoplifting — stealing things from shops
pick it out — here, take it out (of your bag)
supermarket — large, self-service food shop

🎧 Exercise 1

Answer each of the following questions quite briefly but using a complete sentence for each answer.

1 Did Mary choose the right person from the identification parade on television?
2 Was she certain that she was right in her choice?
3 What does Doris say happens 'as the days go by'?
4 Is identification enough by itself to prove that someone is guilty?
5 What other sorts of evidence might be used by the police?
6 Do the police ever make mistakes about identification?
7 Would Doris remember exactly what she was doing some weeks previously if a policeman asked her?
8 Why do shoplifters put things in other people's bags in shops?

Exercise 2

Give a brief explanation for each of the following words and phrases as it is used on the tape.

1 I *chose* the right fellow
2 *as the days go by*
3 *What do they go on?*
4 that was the *one* there
5 you need *several people*
6 they've been *proved wrong* lots of times
7 *shoplifting*
8 things like that must be *terrifying*
9 *pick it out* outside
10 *when you're not thinking*

Exercise 3

Using today's date as the starting point, work out the exact date of each of the following.

1 a fortnight ago tonight
2 a week last Friday
3 the Thursday after next
4 two weeks ago
5 Tuesday of the week after next
6 in three weeks' time
7 in three weeks' time next Thursday
8 a week ago
9 on Saturday week
10 this time next year

Exercise 4

In England, there is only one police force. The police have to do a number of different jobs. Add ten more things for which the police are responsible to the list below.

1 looking for criminals
2 taking down information at road accidents

18.3 Ray and Isabel talk over their worries about having children.

The time has come for Ray and Isabel, who are both successful in their jobs, to consider whether to start a family. They have got used to living quite comfortably on their joint income, and have to face the fact that they would live less well on just one income. Ray thinks there are other problems to face, too.

Points of detail
give up work — stop going to work
poverty — being poor
grinds you down — here, pushes you down, depresses you
end up — finish
in terms of trying to achieve happiness — as far as trying to achieve happiness is concerned. Another example: 'In terms of money, I'd be better off keeping my present job.'
counter-productive — not likely to produce the desired results
all-important — the most important thing

the lack of it — not having it
priorities — here, what matters most
the wage-earning parent — the parent who earns the money
accustomed — used to
pressure — here, extra problem
pressures me — is hard enough for me
all aspects — all matters concerned with
upbringing — training and education during childhood
religion — system of faith, attachment to a church
rift — a difference of opinion, a division

Exercise 1

Answer each of the following questions, using a complete sentence for each answer.

1 What worries Isabel about giving up work to have children?
2 Does she expect to enjoy being worse off?
3 Does she consider money above everything else?
4 Does Ray seem sympathetic with her views?
5 Does Ray find his job easy?
6 What other aspect besides money worries Ray?
7 Do Ray and Isabel share the same religious beliefs?
8 Why is Ray worried about the child's religion?

Exercise 2

Use each of the following words in italics in a sentence of your own.

1 we would be able to *afford* it
2 *poverty*
3 trying to *achieve* happiness
4 the *lack* of it can make . . .
5 a difference in *priorities*
6 as a *parent*
7 *earn* more money
8 we've become *accustomed*
9 we're very *truthful* with each other
10 all *aspects* of the child
11 the child's *religion*
12 We will have to *decide*

Exercise 3

Ray and Isabel are worried about the effect having a child may have on their lives. Almost anything can change someone's life. Write down ten things that might happen to you or around you which would have a significant effect on your life.

Can you say . . .?

The list at the beginning of the Unit will give you some phrases to use when you are anxious or worried about things. Talk to your friends about your worries and theirs. The topics below may remind you of things that worry you.
— health
— financial problems
— relationships with other people
— being unemployed
— going into hospital
— difficult neighbours

---

19 People imagining

They say . . .

But I would . . .
If I was ever in a position . . .
I would certainly do so
Would you intervene?
Fear may make me more cautious
It would depend entirely if . . .
I probably wouldn't intervene
But I would think of a way of . . .
I certainly would do something
It would depend too whether . . .
If somebody was . . ., then you really couldn't . . .

I've often imagined myself . . .
I would get very frustrated
I would feel guilty . . .
I think you would have to . . .
If you were paralysed . . ., you would start making things
Perhaps you could start repairing watches
If you found that you could do it
I like to think that I would . . .
One would obviously have to change one's lifestyle
You wouldn't be able to go upstairs
If you were blind . . . there would be a problem
(I) suppose you could get a guide dog

I think we would buy a house
I live in hope that . . .
I think probably (that) what we would do would be to . . .
I think we'd both continue working
We could go to Africa
We'd get ourselves a higher standard of . . .
Would you stop working?
I'd go mad
If I didn't have anything to annoy me, I don't know how
  I'd live

19.1 Colin says what he'd do if he saw someone commit a crime.

We all wonder what we'd do if we saw somebody commit a crime. Most of us never do actually see a crime committed. When Colin did see a major crime committed, he was unsure of what had happened and so was not able to do anything about it. However, if he did see somebody do something that they shouldn't, he would do what he could either to prevent it or to ensure that they were caught.

Points of detail
incident — event, what happened
pay a very high penalty — Colin believes that society suffers a lot from the actions of criminals.
at any rate — here, in any case
intervene — step in, interfere
cautious — careful
get out — Colin imagines himself in a shop and so says he would 'get out', i.e. leave, go out
the attacker — the person attacking someone or committing the crime
armed — had a gun or other thing used to harm others
an axe — a tool used for cutting wood
weapons — things like guns, knives, etc.
beating up — hitting
fists — tightly closed hands
tempted — inclined
grievously — seriously
maimed — lose a limb (a leg or an arm)
lunatic — madman

Exercise 1

Answer each of the following questions using a complete sentence for each answer.

1   What crime has Colin actually seen?
2   Why didn't he do anything about it?
3   What would Colin do if he saw someone committing a crime?
4   Would Colin intervene in a violent crime?
5   What would he do instead of intervening?
6   What is Moira's view on what one should do if the attacker is armed?
7   Would she think the same about an unarmed attacker?

Find the word or phrase on the tape for which each of the following words or phrases in italics is an explanation.

1   *on one occasion* I've seen . . .
2   it happened so *rapidly*
3   I was *definitely* not sure
4   I believe somebody's *taken* something
5   I don't believe in *permitting* people . . .
6   Would you *interfere*?
7   *being afraid* may make me more . . .
8   more *careful*
9   it would depend *completely*
10 to *try* to prevent it
11 the attacker was *carrying a gun*
12 *striking* somebody else

Exercise 3

Colin and Moira use the word 'intervene', meaning to 'come between'. Find the word beginning with 'inter-' for which each of the following is an explanation.

1   time between two events
2   break into (e.g. a conversation)
3   a face to face meeting
4   translate from one language to another
5   between nations
6   question (e.g. a prisoner)
7   situated inside
8   between elementary and advanced

Exercise 4

Explain what each of the following criminals would do by writing a sentence like the one in the example.
Example: A shoplifter would steal things from shops.

1   a bank robber
2   a murderer
3   a kidnapper
4   a smuggler
5   a vandal

19.2 Ray imagines what life would be like if he became physically handicapped.

Ray is perhaps unusual in having thought about what life would be like if he became physically handicapped in some way. Most people believe that it will never happen to them — it only happens to other people. The difficulties often turn out to be large in number but most handicapped people overcome them. Ray thinks of just some of the problems he would have to face.

Points of detail
bound — here, limited, confined, i.e. unable to leave
a wheel-chair — a chair on wheels, used by people who are unable to walk
lost the use of — no longer able to use
struck blind — become blind, i.e. unable to see
frightful — horrifying
paralysed — unable to move
frustrated — here, irritated at not being able to do things
fend for myself — do things for myself
upkeep — maintenance
guilty — here, worried
to support me — here, to keep me, i.e. financially
skills — abilities
from the waist downwards — below the waist
facility — ability
points to the fact — indicates, shows
compensating — here, making up for what they can't do, replacing one thing by another
adjust and adapt — here, change and do things differently
lifestyle — way in which one lives, e.g. 'The Browns have changed their lifestyle since they inherited her father's money.'
guide-dog — a dog which is specially trained to take blind people where they wish to go

ᏧᏇ Exercise 1

Decide whether each of these statements is true or false, according to what Ray and Isabel say.

1 Ray was once bound to a wheel-chair.
2 Ray would rather be in a wheel-chair than blind.
3 Ray wouldn't mind not going to work if he were paralysed.
4 He would feel unhappy about Isabel looking after him.
5 Isabel suggests that a person who can't walk would need to learn new things.

6 Ray's present job is watch-repairing.
7 Ray thinks that if someone loses one sense he develops the others.
8 Isabel would expect to get a guide-dog if Ray was paralysed.

Exercise 2

Complete each of the sentences below in the same pattern as the example.
Example: If I were blind, I wouldn't be able to study electronics.

1 If she was lame, she . . .
2 If you were paralysed from the knees downwards, you . . .
3 If I were deaf, I . . .
4 If he was dumb, he . . .
5 If I were paralysed in both arms, I . . .
6 If I had no sense of touch, I . . .
7 If she couldn't hear, she . . .
8 If you had no sense of taste, you . . .

Exercise 3

Explain each of the phrases below. They are all taken from the tape.

1 having lost the use of my legs
2 having been struck blind
3 a frightful thought
4 I'd really prefer
5 to fend for myself
6 to contribute to the upkeep of the house
7 and work to support me
8 develop new skills
9 repairing (watches)
10 to change one's lifestyle

19.3 Beryl and Tim imagine how they'd spend a fortune.

Most people have day-dreams occasionally about the things they'd do if they were really rich. Beryl and Tim certainly do. Both of them think of the kinds of luxury which they cannot enjoy at present.

Points of detail

Cornwall — the south west tip of England

want out of life — i.e. what they would really like to have

tootle around — colloquial expression for 'travel gently around'

ports — seaside places where boats can stop

Premium Bonds — In England, there is a national lottery with prizes every week. One buys Premium Bonds, which can be kept forever, and each week the owners of the lucky numbers win large sums of money

come home — Tim uses a horse-racing expression, where 'to come home' means 'to win'.

the *Evening Standard* — an evening newspaper sold in London

convinced — sure

uneconomical — expensive, wasteful

a higher standard of *passage de motor-bike* — Tim humorously invents a French-sounding expression to mean 'a better means of transport'.

absurd — silly

drive me crazy — make me mad

Exercise 1

Answer each of the following questions by choosing the most appropriate answer from A B C or D.

1 Beryl's children would especially like
A to live in Cornwall   C to live in a new house
B to have some horses   D to have a yacht

2 Beryl and her husband, Dave, want a yacht because
A the girls want horses
B they don't like living in a house
C they'd like to travel about by sea
D they tootle around Cornwall

3 Tim hopes to get a fortune by
A asking the *Evening Standard*
B living in London
C buying some Premium Bonds
D winning a Premium Bond prize

4 Tim's first thought, if he won a fortune, would be
A to travel much more   C to buy a Premium Bond
B to live in London   D to go to work more

5 Tim thinks international travel is
A very difficult   C not difficult
B cheap   D tiring

6 Tim doesn't go to South East Asia now because of
   A difficulties   C the distance
   B the price   D his short holidays

7 Tim mentions three methods of transport. Which of the
   following does he *not* mention?
   A a helicopter   C a car
   B a motor-bike   D a yacht

8 Tim
   A would   C might
   B wouldn't   D couldn't
   give up work if he won a fortune.

Exercise 2

*Find the word or phrase on the tape for which each of the
following words or phrases in italics is an explanation.*

1   which we like *especially* well
2   I would buy a *sailing boat*
3   I always *examine* the Evening Standard
4   I'm *certain* it's me
5   we'd both *go on* working
6   all the *free* time we had
7   international travel is fairly *easy*
8   the obvious one of *price*
9   a *better quality* of 'passage de motor-bike'
10 *foolish* things that money can buy

Exercise 3

*Write a paragraph about what you'd do if you won a fortune.
First decide on the sum of money — you can make it as large
as you like! Begin:*
Amount: £ . . . .
If I won £ . . . ., I'd . . . .

Can you say . . .?

Now go back to the list at the beginning of the Unit. You will find lots of expressions to help you imagine what you'd do if . . . Take some of the topics below and let your imagination run wild! Tell your friends what you'd do and ask them what they'd do.

— if you saw a crime
— to get a lot of money
— if you lost your car/bicycle/etc.
— if you saw someone drowning
— to change the appearance of your house
— if you wanted to find a wife/husband

20 People making plans

> **They say . . .**
>
> What do you want?
> I'd like to go to . . .
> We could go for a meal
> Let's go to a restaurant
> I always wanted to . . .
> We always seem to end up going to . . .
>
> If you like, I'll pick Margaret and Chris up tomorrow
> Then I could take them . . .
> Well, . . . I could stay for tea and then . . .
> Perhaps their friends could take them back
> That would be the best idea, wouldn't it?
> What I could do is take them to you and then . . .
> And then, I could come back
> What time would it be best to . . .?
> Probably about four o'clock
> Would that be a suitable suggestion?
> That would mean I needn't . . .
>
> What about tomorrow?
> Can I look in my diary?
> Tomorrow's not on
> When will you be back?
> I will be passing through, if you can let me know . . .
> Then I'll be able to plan . . .
> You can wait till Tuesday and go back . . .
> I just couldn't come during the day in the week
> Good days are Saturdays and Sundays
> I'm going to join a hockey club
> What about time?

20.1 Sarah, Lucy and Avril try to plan an evening out.

The three girls are trying to decide how they'd like to spend
an evening which Mary is going to pay for. They don't make

much progress because they get distracted by discussing what they think of all the alternatives they consider.

Points of detail
appeals — seems attractive
theatre production — here, Sarah means a straight play
dull patches — here, a period which is uninteresting (because there are no good films on)
Walt Disney cartoons — lighthearted films made by photographing series of drawings, made famous by Walt Disney
Oscars — prizes given in America for the best films of the year
such and such — here, a particular film
end up — finish
the company — the people you are with

Exercise 1

Answer each of the following questions, using a brief sentence for each answer.

1 Does Sarah prefer drama or musicals?
2 Avril would like to go to the cinema, but there is a problem about that. What is it?
3 Who makes films which children like?
4 Why are there a lot of children's films on?
5 What three kinds of restaurant does Avril mention?
6 Why does Sarah usually go to Italian restaurants?
7 What restaurants does Lucy like?
8 What does Sarah say influences how much she enjoys going to a restaurant?

Exercise 2

Find the word or phrase on the tape for which each of the following words and phrases in italics is an explanation.

1 the theatre *is attractive*
2 it's so *dear*
3 so *difficult* to get to see ...
4 *I'd rather* see a musical
5 one of those *uninteresting* patches
6 I can't *recollect* what
7 big *famous* films
8 ... *lately* that I've noticed
9 *What kind of* restaurant?
10 perhaps if I'm *not pleased after all*

Exercise 3

Listen to Exercise 3 on your tape and write down what Sarah says.

Exercise 4

List at least ten other things the girls could have considered doing for their evening out.

20.2 Ray and Julia make arrangements about giving some friends a lift.

Julia is expecting some visitors, Margaret and Chris, but they don't have a car and there are problems about how to get them to Julia's house and then home again. The matter is made more complicated by the fact that the visitors want to go on to someone else's house when they leave Julia's.

Points of detail

Sunbury — a small town to the west of London
Effingham — another small town; where Margaret and Chris live
taxi them — drive them
sitting around — sitting doing nothing
find their own way back — i.e. find their own method of getting back
pick them up — collect them
quite a way — i.e. quite a long way
meeting point — place to meet
miss them — here, not see them

Exercise 1

Decide whether each of these statements is true or false, according to the planning that Ray and Julia have done.

1 Ray is to collect Margaret and Julia tomorrow.
2 Margaret and Chris live in Sunbury.
3 They have friends in Sunbury.
4 Margaret and Chris have already arranged transport from Sunbury to Effingham.
5 Ray volunteers to drive them from Sunbury to Effingham.
6 Isabel suggests that the friends in Sunbury can take Margaret and Chris home.
7 Ray will take Isabel home.

8   Ray suggests picking Margaret and Chris up at five o'clock.
9   It's not far from Effingham to Sunbury.
10 Margaret has offered to meet Ray somewhere else other than her house.

Exercise 2

Use each of the following phrases from the tape as the beginning of a sentence of your own.

1   Well, if you like . . .
2   I could take . . .
3   The trouble is . . .
4   If you don't mind . . .
5   I've got the time . . .
6   What I could do is . . .
7   We could stay and . . .
8   It's quite a way . . .
9   We will have finished . . .
10 Margaret did say . . .

Exercise 3

Put the following list in the order in which it is planned to occur.

1   Ray will take Margaret and Chris to Julia's house.
2   Ray will take Isabel home.
3   Ray will take Margaret and Chris to Sunbury.
4   Ray will pick up Margaret and Chris.
5   Margaret and Chris will visit friends in Sunbury.
6   Ray will come back to Julia's house alone.
7   Julia will give everyone tea.
8   They will have a few more drinks.

Exercise 4

Make a list of things you are going to do tomorrow and from your list tell someone what you intend to do. The expressions at the beginning of the Unit will be useful.

20.3 Mary tries to plan another meeting with Graham, Tim O. and Nigel.

Mary wants to fix a day and a time when Graham, Tim and Nigel can come to her house again. There are all sorts of problems, particularly because it's a holiday week-end and the three young men are busy people.

Points of detail
not on — here, not possible, a colloquial use of 'on'
with the lads — all the young men together
accordingly — according to what other arrangements I've made
open — for a ticket, this means without a fixed date for the journey
hit London — colloquial for 'arrive in London'
inter-company van — a van owned by a group of companies which
    travels between their various offices, factories, etc.
rugby — a game rather like soccer, but played with an oval-shaped
    ball which can be handled
hockey — a game played by teams of 11 players with a small hard
    ball and hockey sticks on a field rather like a football pitch

Exercise 1

Answer the following questions by choosing the most appropriate answer from A B C or D.

1   Tomorrow is only perhaps possible for
    A Mary   C Tim
    B Graham   D Nigel

2   Nigel and Graham have arranged a night out
    A with other young men   C with Tim
    B with Bridget   D on their own

3   Tim will be back from his holidays
    A for Christmas
    B at the end of December
    C in the first week of January
    D tomorrow

4   Tim has a ticket for his return journey which
    A will only get him home
    B will only get him to London
    C will only get him to the English coast
    D will only be useful before Christmas

5 Tim has an open ticket, which means he
   A can go anywhere   C cannot travel any day
   B can only travel in London   D can travel any day

6 Graham can only come at week-ends or in the evenings
   because
   A he wants to play rugby   C he works in the week
   B he lives in London   D he wants to join a hockey
                                 club

7 Rugby is the game played by
   A Tim   C Graham
   B Nigel   D Mary

8 Graham is going to join
   A a rugby game   C a hockey club
   B a holiday club   D a hockey match

Exercise 2

*Find a word which rhymes with each of these words. If you
are not sure of the sound of a word you can find it on the
tape. Write a sentence which includes the word you have
found.*
Example: tomorrow
Possible answer: When the cat died, I was filled with
                 sorrow.

1	right	5	van
2	lad	6	nice
3	Tim	7	day
4	advance	8	club

Exercise 3

*Put a correct preposition in each of the following expressions
of time.*

1 He came here . . . . Monday.
2 I'll see you . . . . the week-end
3 Meet me here on the Monday . . . . next.
4 He was here last week but he'd gone . . . . the week-
   end.
5 I'll have finished . . . . Wednesday.

166

6 We should have completed the decorations . . . . a
month from now.
7 I can't come . . . . Christmas, I'll come afterwards.
8 Please ring me . . . . the Tuesday, not before.

Can you say . . .?

Look back at the expressions at the beginning of the Unit.
They will help you when you are planning something, but
there are many other expressions, especially expressions of
time and place, which you will probably use as well. Try
making plans with a friend about any, or all, of these
things:
— to meet next week
— to go to the swimming-pool
— to play football at a club
— to borrow something and return it
— to look at a house you'd like to buy
— to arrange an end of course party for the class
— to arrange what the class will do next week now
that you've finished this book . . .